Naked Frailties

This book is dedicated
to my childhood friend Ellice Watson
and her husband Wilby (Sonny),
who have been constant and sincere
in their friendship and love.

Naked Frailties

Short stories, poetry, and articles

Linda M. Brissett

Briss Books, Inc.
Hamilton, 1999

Canadian Cataloguing in Publication Data

Brissett, Linda M.
      Naked frailties: short stories, poetry, and articles

ISBN 0-9699369-2-3

      I. Title.

PS8553.R547N34 1999   C811'.54   C99-900571-5
PR9199.3.B6938N34 1999

Published by Briss Books, Inc.
58 Skyview Drive
Hamilton, Ontario   L9B 1X5

Desgin by Gilda Mekler; production by Mekler & Deahl, Publishers
Printed by Transcontinental

Acknowledgements

I would like to acknowledge with gratitude my good friend Dr. Alezandre Dauphin, for taking time out of his very busy schedule to read the manuscript and write the foreword for this book.

Information Sources

For the article "April is No Fools' Month": *Merit Student Encyclopedia, Volume 2*, 1993, pages 62-63; *Webster's New World Dictionary, 2nd College Edition*, page 68.

For the articles "Black Canadians — Part of the Canadian Family Tree," and "Some Black Canadian Firsts": "The Canadian Family Tree: Canada's People." Multicultural Directorate, Dept.of Secretary of State, *Corpus*, Toronto, 1980.

The content of the article "Tiny Victims of Drug Abuse" is based on the author's experience in the care of newborns, and a personal survey, in which 21 babies born to smoking and drug-abusing mothers were studied over a one-month period.

Foreword

Poetry can be said to be the voice of that wandering spirit who comes to rest in flesh in characters and sounds that are intriguing to mankind. Mrs. L. Brissett is a poet whose diversity brings, in this compilation of works, a tropical fruit punch prepared in an unpredictable, cold climate, yet to be savoured by many. From the almost-reality of a dream which stimulates our sympathetic system to the admiration of nature in its evolution, this bouquet of short stories and poetry expresses the sentiment of a world wherein our existence is palpable.

Life is renewed through strife and confession. The naïveté of childhood and the cruelty of adulthood are visited. Love is sung to its different tunes. Appreciation is worded with the most intimate feelings. Family is praised with the charming beat of love and pride; and so much more.

It is my hope that this potpourri of concrete emotions with such a universal taste will vibrate the chords of our memories as we absorb the resonance of this poet.

Alezandre Dauphin, MD

Table of Contents

Introduction

Many of the pieces in *Naked Frailties* expose some of the ugliness and disappointments of life, which most of us are inclined to ignore or reject, pretending they do not exist and will never exist, as long as we tell ourselves that they don't. We revel in the joys and pleasures of life and its seasons, the beauty and awe of nature, and the wonder of our strengths.

No one is eager to acknowledge the darker sides of life. We would much rather dwell on the pleasant and more palatable things, until we are suddenly confronted in a profound way with reality.

Some of the stories, poems, and articles in this book deal openly with some of humankind's frailties — lost youth, lost health, prejudice and injustice, anger, hatred, and death. At the same time, others point out our ability to enjoy life: to wonder at nature and admire its beauty in every form. It is like looking at our own naked form in the mirror for the first time, and seeing and accepting the many flaws and weaknesses while accepting the beauty and the strengths. We do not like the flaws, but they are part of us and we have to accept them and try to live with them to the best of our abilities.

Not all of us are willing to be candid about our feelings regarding such things as aging, death, prejudice, social injustice, and even love. This book is trying to show that it is perfectly all right to be angry, to show fear, to abhor lies and injustices, as long as we deal with them in a rational, civilized manner. We have to acknowledge that they are a part of the package of living and we must confront them and accept them as things we are not able to change or control.

Only through facing and accepting the inevitable can we realize the ability of the human spirit to triumph over the fear of the unknown. Then we may even be able to laugh at our frailties, rather than mourn the loss of our strengths.

Short Stories, Not Tall Tales

TO DREAM A REALITY

*L*ouisa felt a presence and opened her eyes to find Miss Minna looking down at her.

Louisa had fallen asleep lying supine, with her right arm resting on her forehead. She sat up quickly, swung her legs over the side of the bed, and gave a start as her feet touched the cold linoleum floor.

Miss Minna stepped back when her daughter-in-law sat up.

"Did you hear what happened?" she asked in a soft, bewildered-sounding voice. She looked about the small bedroom nervously, and then directly at Louisa, who was still a bit dazed from the effects of sleep.

"No!" Louisa answered, trying hard to focus. "What happened?"

She did not understand what this was all about. As far as she knew, Miss Minna had left for her country home in Maggoty last night, and should be just about nearing there.

Her mother-in-law had spent last Saturday with Ossie and Louisa before going on to visit her eldest son Brad in Constant Spring. From there she had left last night for her home, after a one-week visiting blitz with her three sons and their families.

Shortly after they had made love, her husband had gotten dressed and gone to see his mother off at the station. He had wanted her to accompany him, but she had declined and stayed in bed, as she always liked to do after making love. Unlike Ossie, who could get up and go right away, she seemed to have the need to savour the feeling.

Now Louisa thought, *If Miss Minna left last night for home, what is she doing here in our apartment in the middle of the night asking if I heard about something?* She told herself that Minna might have missed her train, and whatever she wanted to tell her must be very important for her to come at this hour. She must have come by taxi, although it is not unusual in Jamaica for people to

3

walk for miles to get to where they want to go if there is no transportation.

Avoiding her eyes, Miss Minna skirted Louisa's question and asked another.

"Would you like to go see for yourself?" Without knowing what she was going to see or why, Louisa nodded.

"Okay, come." Miss Minna turned and walked through the door.

Louisa followed, closing the door behind her without looking back. It did not occur to her to awaken Ossie and let him in on this somewhat unsettling event.

She moved down the steps from the verandah and onto the dusty yard. Her mother-in-law was already at the gate and going through it. Louisa hurried and caught up with her as she moved west on Barry Street.

Someone coughed noisily behind her. The sound came from the west wall of Barnes Gully, which bordered Number Two Barry Street, where she lived. Louisa did not turn to see who had coughed. It was no doubt the rastafarian named Founder, who, it was known, frequented that area especially to smoke ganja. The pungent odour found her nostrils and made her sneeze.

Miss Minna was many strides ahead of her and she found it difficult to keep up with her. In fact she found that the older woman was always walking slightly ahead of her.

The night was illumined by a new moon, which shone through a clear tropical sky, and the warm August air was fanned by a cool refreshing breeze, the kind that is usually associated with the Christmas season.

The streets were deserted except for the two women, and the only sounds heard, apart from their footsteps, were the occasional barking of dogs.

Louisa had tried twice to make conversation, not only to break the silence between them but also to see if Miss Minna would slow her pace a bit. But she never responded. She seemed bent on an urgent mission. She did, however, look back over her shoulder at intervals to make sure Louisa was still following.

It seemed rather strange that the older woman, who was usually very talkative, had abandoned speech for speed. And what was even more unusual was the fact that Louisa was following her in the dead of night fully dressed without being aware of ever having changed out of her nightclothes before leaving the apartment.

This was the fourth time that Louisa had seen Ossie's mother. She was a believer in good morals and had been blunt in her letters, stating that she would not visit them as long as they "continued to live in sin." She had kept her word. After fourteen months of living together, Ossie and Louisa had gotten married before Justice of the Peace Jude Russell. She was twenty-three, and two months pregnant.

Miss Minna had visited them for the first time a week after the ceremony. She had brought them fresh garden produce, some corned pork, and two chickens to be raised for their eggs, all from the family farm.

Both women had taken to each other immediately. Unlike Ossie's father, who had visited them on numerous occasions before, his mother was less critical of Louisa and offered her moral support. She gave her valuable advice regarding pre- and postnatal care for herself and her baby. By the time the visit was over, the two had become very close. Miss Minna was now the parent Louisa had lost to death at age three.

Life with Oswald Nehmiah was good even if they were poor. They were always able to manage and they loved each other dearly. Ossie worked as a conductor on the JOS buses, and in the last six months had gotten his own route, which meant better working hours.

Louisa worked as a steno-typist at Ryma-Lynde Associates at King and Harbour Streets, a job she loved but which did not pay well.

When little Gladstone was born everything seemed perfect. The world was a fairyland with the three of them in it, and love and laughter was unlimited.

Then four months ago, when the baby was three months old, tragedy had struck.

Louisa had gone back to work a few weeks before in order to augment Ossie's salary. The baby was left at the creche in the mornings on her way to work, and picked up at four in the afternoons.

The slanting rays of a low sun had fired the heaped clouds

of the April evening with flame, making the air unbearably warm and humid. As Louisa carried her baby home from the creche, she had sensed that something was wrong. He had felt strangely tense in her arms and had appeared very sleepy.

At first the young mother had put it down to the intense heat of the day, but by the time they got home she knew something was wrong. Gladstone refused to fix and suck when she tried to breastfeed him. Then in the middle of his diaper change she noticed his eyes rolling backwards. He stiffened and then convulsed.

There had been a loud, piercing scream, but Louisa was not aware that it had come from her. Her neighbours had rallied and in a jiffy she was in the back of a taxi holding the quiet bundle that was her baby.

When they arrived at the Emergency Room, a nurse had taken the bundle from her and hurried into a screened cubicle. There had been a flurry of activities around her and she began to feel faint. Someone had helped her into an easy chair and placed a wet towel on her forehead. A male voice behind the screen had said, "This is a DOA."

Then Ossie was there! He had cupped her face briefly then dashed behind the screen where the action was.

"Oh my God! Help him! Help him!" He had shouted. And somewhere in the distance a voice had uttered "… came in dead. There's nothing we can do now ... post mortem to find out the cause."

In the twinkling of an eye the Nehmiahs' fairyland had crumbled to dust.

Miss Minna had come again. Not only was she a source of comfort to the young couple in their grief, but she defended Louisa when her father-inlaw blamed her for going back to work too soon and leaving his grandchild in the care of "incompetent people."

It was found out later that the baby had suffered brain injury from a fall, most likely at the creche, but no one ever admitted to being responsible.

After a week, the older Nehmiahs had returned to the country and left the young people to carry on with life. It was tough and the hurting sometimes was unbearable, but they tried to cope. They made love often and passionately as if some unknown force was willing them towards another conception. In fact Louisa thought she was pregnant again, but decided to delay telling Ossie until she was sure.

Then last week, out of the blue, Miss Minna had decided to come to town again and spend some time with each of her children and their families. It was a spur of the moment thing, she had said when she visited them last Saturday. And as usual, the time spent with her mother-in-law was peaceful and inspiring. They talked about anything and everything, and as was her way, Miss Minna left her with a quote from the Bible — *Consider the lilies of the field how they grow.*

It was obvious that Miss Minna had not left for the country, for here she was, traversing the length of Barry Street so bent on revealing something to her daughter-in-law that conversation was nonexistent.

They had now turned left off Barry Street onto Pechong Street and headed for the Jamaica Government Railway Station where Pechong Street ended. A rasta man dressed in khaki shorts and a white T-shirt was pushing an oversized handcart towards the station, on the other side of the street.

Louisa followed closely behind the older woman, and entered the deserted building. They went onto the platform, where a passenger train was waiting. Miss Minna looked at her daughter-in-law and ordered "Follow me. It won't be long now."

Louisa felt a warm sticky feeling around and under her breasts. She moved her hand across her nipples and found that her blouse and bra were soaked. There had been other occasions when her breasts would fill up and leak whenever she thought of her dead baby.

Oh, fathers, she thought. *I haven't got anything to put into my bra to absorb this. I am going to be soaked by the time I get back home!*

She entered the dark empty compartment with Miss Minna and sat by the window beside her. The train pulled out almost immediately and went at a fair speed.

There still was no conversation between them, but Louisa had adjusted to the strange situation she had found herself in. She stared instead, at the montages of ghostly shapes and shadows that flew by her window as the journey progressed. After a short while a whistle sounded, and the train slowed and stopped. Miss Minna was on her feet instantly.

"Come on!" she said without looking back. They stepped from the train onto a grassy path, lined on either side by trees and tall pampas grass. The smell of jasmine was overpowering, but there was also the sickly smell of blood. They continued unhindered down the path as the sounds of a myriad crickets and bullfrogs filled the night and made it much more eerie. The ground and bushes around them were wet, maybe from a recent downpour.

The moon came out from behind the clouds and stayed, flooding the countryside with its brilliance. And the path came to an abrupt end. Miss Minna slowly turned to face Louisa and said "There! This is what happened."

Louisa froze in horror at what her eyes were seeing. There was death and destruction all around them. Bodies and body parts were strewn about over a wide area as far as she could see. Mangled metal and wood as well as uprooted and splintered trees were everywhere. Above them and to the right, the forward engine of the train, with one coach still attached, hung precariously over the edge of the precipice. A brown-skinned man in peaked cap stood crushed between the steering wheel and rear walls of the engine. His hands seemed fixed to the steering wheel and his eyes stared into the darkness.

The mangled coaches seemed to form a fractured line down the hillside, eventually disappearing into the gorge, whose waters could be heard rushing wildly into the deep dark distance.

Hundreds of bodies, some missing heads and limbs, littered the area. The devastation in Louisa's mind was akin to the ending of the world — Armageddon. She was overcome by a surge of nausea, and vomited in a sage bush.

"Come," Miss Minna said softly, touching her lightly on the shoulder. "Let's go back."

They moved quickly back up the path and into the waiting train. Again they were alone and there was no conversation. Louisa closed her eyes and tried to block out the horrible pictures that were vivid in her mind, but with no success. *Thank God*, she thought, *that Miss Minna had not gone back last night.*

And then they were back at her apartment. She was not even aware of the journey from the railway station in Kingston to her home, but was glad it had ended.

Miss Minna stepped back and allowed her daughter-in-law to enter the bedroom first. Louisa glanced at her sleeping husband and realized that he had not even known she had gone.

She sat on the side of the bed and looked at Miss Minna, who was still standing. She was about to say aloud what she was thinking: *I'm glad you were not on that train last night.*

Then she began to see her mother-in-law in a clearer, more focused light. She was wearing a white dress with green polka-dots, with a sweetheart neckline and peplum frill at the waist. The dress emphasized her petite form.

The front of the dress was saturated with a deep dark red, which appeared to be still damp. Louisa could not see her mother-in-law's left arm, and the sleeve of the dress hung limply from her shoulder.

"Oh my God, no!" Louisa gasped.

"Yes!" said Miss Minna. "I'm sorry. I didn't have time. I lost my breasts and left leg too. I have to go back and find them." With that she vanished.

"No!" cried Louisa. *"Nooo!"* she screamed, as she sat up in bed and realized that she had been asleep. Her screams awakened Ossie. Seeing the horror in her eyes, he held her close and soothingly said, "You were having a bad dream, honey, it's all right now." The front of her nightgown was wet and seeped through his pyjama shirt. The warm, sticky feeling of his wife's milk coating his chest hairs aroused him, and he wanted to make love to her. But she became hysterical.

"She's dead!" She cried. "Your mother is dead! They're all dead. The train crashed. It fell over a precipice." Ossie grabbed her shoulder and shook her. "Stop it! Stop it!" he said, hoping this would calm her into some sense of rationality. It did. Her screams subsided into a low moan.

"Honey, you had a bad dream," he coaxed. He looked into her eyes and saw the horror there.

"The front of her dress was soaked with blood right down to the peplum at the waist. You could barely tell that it was green polka-dot ..."

Ossie stiffened. His wife was describing in mournful tones the dress that his mother had been wearing when she boarded the train last night. How could she have known? She was asleep when he got back from the station! He pulled away from her, looked at her face and saw reality in her eyes. He stretched across to the far side of the bed and switched on the radio. The neighbourhood roosters were heralding the dawn.

"This is ZQI Jamaica, 3.48 ..." There was some static in the set and he adjusted it until the sound was clear again. "... in shock," the voice of the newscaster continued "at the terrible, terrible disaster, the first in Jamaica's rail history. The accident is reported to have occurred at about 2.53 this morning. The rear engine and most of the coaches are lying in a tangled heap at the bottom of the gorge near Balaclava. None of the three hundred and fifteen passengers and crew aboard survived.

"It is reported that bodies, many of them dismembered in the crash, have been strewn over large areas at and beyond the crash site. Landslides due to recent rains are thought ..."

"Oh, my God! Oh, my God! Oh, my God!" Ossie's heart-rending screams and Louisa's low mournful sobbing made a sorrowful duet, which came from the deepest chasms of their souls. They held each other closely as they sobbed, and rocked back and forth, back and forth, back and forth ...

THE MORASS POND

*J*asper Bryden dropped his bicycle on the driveway. He looked curiously at the small figure that moved quickly through the grassy fields, across the road from his house. He wiped his forehead with the back of his hands, sweeping his hair from his eyes. Blinking, he looked again across the street, not wanting to lose sight of what held his interest. The person was quickly disappearing from view.

"Jasper, get that bike off the driveway now."

He turned to face his mother, who was vigorously shaking a small rug.

"Haven't I told you not to leave your bike on the driveway? If you are finished with it, please put it away."

She shook the rug some more, then went back into the house, leaving a cloud of dust behind her.

Grasping the bike by its handlebars, Jasper stood it on its wheels and walked it into the backyard. He leaned it against the house, then ran down to the sidewalk.

Shading his eyes with his hands, he scanned the fields. There was no one walking by now. He became tense with excitement. He knew that was Michael Marne, his next-door neighbor, with whom he was no longer allowed to play. Jasper had seen him walking through the fields last Wednesday, and had thought nothing of it. Yesterday he had seen him coming back carrying a jar. There was something moving in the water, but he was too far away to see what it was.

Jasper had been curious about the contents of the jar, but his mother had been with him.

Michael was eight years old, two years younger than Jasper, but taller and slimmer. He had fair hair and fair skin, with freckles on his nose. Michael had owned a brown and black German Shepherd dog named Bull, a bone of contention between the two families. The dog was accustomed to barking a lot whenever he was leashed. The Brydens' complaints always fell on deaf ears. Then one day in the Marnes' absence, Bull somehow got onto the road and was killed by a car.

Michael's parents had accused the Brydens of deliberately letting the dog out and causing its death. The families had then become sworn enemies. That was two years ago. The boys since then had eyed each other from a distance, each pretending the other did not exist.

⤳

Jasper's curiosity was getting the better of him. Although he had been warned never to go into the field, he was desperate to know what his young neighbour was up to, and intended to find out.

He checked to make sure that his mother was nowhere in sight, then dashed across the road and onto the footpath that led into the field.

The midmorning air was warm and still and the sky was a distilled blue. Jasper wiped the perspiration from his face with his shirt, as he hurried along. He wished he had worn his cap to shield his head from the sun's rays.

Moving the waist-high grass out of his way with his hands, he pressed onward. He thought of turning back when he did not see Michael. He wanted to get home before his mother could miss him. But his curiosity got the better of him and prompted him to explore the area while he could. Michael might have gone back home for all he knew. This would leave the way open for him to explore.

He felt a familiar burning sensation in his nostrils and gently massaged the top of his nose, hoping for some relief.

The grass began to thin out now, making the path easier to follow, and before long he reached a wooded area, which could not be seen from the road. The cones and needles from the pine trees growing there carpeted the ground. There was a large pond at the foot of a mossy slope. It was filled with floating vegetation.

Wow! This is great, he thought, looking excitedly about him.

"A neat place to come and catch frogs," he said aloud "I bet there are tons of frogs in there!"

"Get away from my pond, or I'll tell my dad!"

Startled, Jasper jumped back and looked up towards the tree under which he stood, into the angry eyes of Michael, who was coming down in great haste.

He had forgotten about Michael and had wrongly assumed that he had gone home. But there he was, as large as life, sliding down the trunk of the tree with ease.

"What d'you want? Get away from my pond, or I'll sock you!"

Michael stood before Jasper, eyes blazing. His nose was sunburnt and peeling. Dirt streaked his face, emphasizing his pale blue eyes. His jaws jerked as he confronted his enemy. His mud-stained blue jeans were rolled up above his knees and the laces of his wet running shoes were undone. Bits of leaves similar to those seen floating in the pond clung to his bare arms. Jasper knew that he must have been wading in the pond, a risky thing to do if one couldn't swim. They eyed each other for a moment.

"Get away, I tell you. Only my friends can play with my frogs, and you're not my friend!" Michael took a step towards Jasper. His fists were clenched and his face set in angry determination. Jasper stepped back towards the pond and stared at Michael.

"But I could be your friend," he coaxed, trying to calm his opponent. The burning sensation in his nostrils was now severe, and he had a headache. Rubbing his nose gently, he continued slowly and cautiously.

"We could play with my ..."

"I don't want to play with you!" Michael's blue eyes flashed. "My mom says I'm not to play with you."

"Who cares about your stinking pond anyway?" Jasper shouted, picking up a pine cone and tossing it into the pond.

"The pond's dirty anyway and has bulrushes in it."

"It's not bulrushes either!" Michael retorted, glancing at the pond protectively. "It's morass. My dad says it grows in morass ponds everywhere."

"That's not morass, stupid! You're stupid, so's your dad and ..." Before he could say anymore, Michael had landed a staggering blow to the side of Jasper's face, shouting as he hit him, "You take that back!"

Tears filled Jasper's eyes uncoaxed and his nostrils felt full. He tried to defend himself but his blows landed softer than

Michael's did. At last he broke free and with all the strength he could muster, pushed him away.

Michael fell back, rolling down the grassy slope and landed in the pond with a splash. Jasper watched in horror as his neighbour disappeared below the surface.

"Michael!" he shouted, running in haste to the edge of the pond and peering in. "I didn't mean to push you in. Michael!"

Just then, Michael surfaced, spluttering and thrashing about, a terrified look on his face. He tried to speak but swallowed water, then disappeared below the surface again.

Jasper looked at the pond in shocked disbelief. Its ripples were spreading outward in ever-widening circles towards the edges. The morass floated lazily, bobbing rhythmically on the water's surface, and blood flowed freely from his nose.

Frantic with fear, and burdened with guilt, he turned and ran from the pond. Blood splashed about on his clothes, as fire burned in his head. In a fleeting moment of rational thought, he realized that he must hurry. He had to get help for Michael and himself.

⌒

Jasper pinched his nose in an effort to stem the bleeding. He ran haltingly through the tall, sun-baked grass towards some trees on the other side of the field. He could hear the frantic splashing in the pond behind him and pictured Michael struggling to keep afloat.

The sun was hot and hazy, and hung midway in the sky. He had pinched his nose like this many times before and the bleeding had stopped at once. But this time it was different. He could feel the warm trickle of blood going past his throat, and was forced to swallow.

Though he was older than Michael, Jasper was shorter and less athletic. His light brown eyes, now dulled with pain, were the only bright spark in a pale, thin face. His full lips, now cracked and dry, often gave the impression that he was pouting. Unlike Michael, he was a good swimmer and regretted now not having tried to help instead of running away.

He stopped for a second and looked back, but could no

longer see the pond, though its exact location was vivid in his mind. He felt faint and nauseated, and wished that he was home. His parents would give him hell for going to the pond, for even talking to Michael, let alone getting into a fight with him.

But now Michael was back there, drowning! Hot tears bathed Jasper's cheeks and moistened the congealed blood in the corners of his mouth.

He stumbled into the shade of the trees and sat down, resting his head against the nearest one. He closed his eyes. Releasing his nose when he thought the bleeding had checked, he sniffed lightly. The blood came streaming down again.

"Help me, Dad!" he cried in a hoarse whisper. "I didn't mean for him to drown, truly I didn't." With that he was engulfed in darkness.

Jasper awoke with a start, groaning as he sat up. He shielded his eyes with his hands. The nosebleed had stopped but the headache persisted, and his face and hands felt sticky and dirty. He stumbled across the field, still weak and confused. He thought he was heading home, but found himself back at the pond.

The water was still, as stagnant ponds usually are, and there was no sign of Michael. He noticed a small pool of water and fronds of weed from the pond on the ground near the foot of a tree. He did not think that was there before, but he couldn't be certain, and he was too sick and weak to care.

He lay down on his side under the tree, then rolled over onto his back. His head rested in the small puddle. It felt cool and soothing. Drifting off into darkness again, he thought he heard voices calling his name and footsteps stomping about near his head. He wanted to answer, but his tongue felt too heavy and sore. He felt strong arms clutching his body, as if a giant had picked him up and was carrying him away. He felt light and helpless as he slowly drifted off.

⟡

Jasper opened his eyes slowly and tried to focus. His eyes ached inside their heavy lids. Trying to raise his right hand to his face, he discovered that it wouldn't move. It was being held by someone's hand, soft and warm and reassuring. He knew that touch very well, and suddenly felt relief and comfort in its touch. He forced his eyes open and looked into the warmth of his mother's eyes. Her face, streaked with her mascara, told him that she had been crying. She was sitting on the side of his bed. Bed?

His mother saw the questioning look in his eyes and said gently. "You're in the hospital, honey. You were dehydrated and had lost a lot of blood. If it wasn't for Michael we might have lost you." She stroked his face with a finger and continued to hold his right hand with hers.

"That's your third bottle of blood." His eyes followed hers to the bottle of red liquid hanging from a metal pole above his bed. It dripped into his right arm through a length of tubing attached to the hanging bottle. He tried to lift his head so he could focus better, but it felt too heavy to move.

"But Michael drowned, Mom!" Jasper said in a whisper, his throat hurting a bit from the effort.

"No, dear," his mother replied gently. "Michael is fine. He is in the waiting room with his parents and your dad. He managed to pull himself out of the pond and found you unconscious in the field. He ran home and alerted his parents. It was his father who brought you out to the road."

The tears stung as he began to sob. "Mom," he whispered painfully. "Michael saved my life, and I killed his dog." Melodie Bryden gasped in disbelief.

"What are you saying, son? What did you do?" She tried not to sound alarmed, but was. Here was her only child, inflicted with this godawful blood disease which almost took his life today, and would have but for the good heart and common sense of young Michael. And now Jasper was confessing to having been responsible for the death of their neighbour's dog!

"What happened, Jasper?" she asked softly, lifting his head off the pillow and cradling it in her arms. "What happened that day?"

"I didn't mean to let him out," Jasper whispered against her neck. "I went in their backyard to get my ball, and couldn't get the latch back on. Bull ran out while I was trying and a car hit him. I am sorry."

Melodie was taken aback by the shocking revelation. She thought of the feuding and unpleasantness between the Marnes and her family, which seemed to have gone on forever, until today when near tragedy brought them together. She realized now that her neighbours' accusations were correct. If only she had known then what she knew now! She felt a deep sense of shame and regret.

"Why didn't you tell us about this before, Jasper?" his mother asked, as she dried his eyes with her sodden handkerchief and tried to comfort him.

"I was scared, Mom." he said, feeling totally drained. "I'll tell them when I'm better."

"Yes, dear," she consoled. "We'll tell them together. Now I'll go and bring them in. They've been waiting for hours to see you."

Jasper watch with relief as the five people walked into the room. They were smiling and seemed at ease with each other.

"Look son," his father said, pulling up a chair for Michael's mother. "Michael has brought you some flowers." He saw a small, sunburnt hand holding a bunch of wild daisies to his face, as he drifted off to sleep. There was a feeling of peacefulness in the room and within. The morass pond was not really that bad after all. It had found him a friend.

Nobody's Grandma

Grandma took off her glasses and wiped them with the hem of her dress. She replaced them on her face and listened intently to the beating wings and loud squawking of the birds at the feeder.

Dennis watched her through the narrow opening of his bedroom door. He smiled to himself. Any moment now he knew she would go out to the sun deck to see what was happening to the birds. "My birds," she referred to them. *As if she had hatched them from her very own eggs,* he thought. He conjured in his mind a blue jay with grey hair on its head instead of feathers. It had miniature slippers on its feet like the ones Grandma wore, and it flew around with them on. He giggled softly to himself, slapping his side in mischievous glee.

He looked through the crack of his door again and, just as he had hoped, Grandma was making her way downstairs. She carried herself elegantly. That was one thing Dennis secretly admired about Grandma: even in her autumn years, she carried herself with grace. She moved at a fair gallop for a woman in her seventies. Dennis knew she was going to investigate the commotion outside. He opened the window that overlooked the sun deck and the bird feeder.

Grandma was especially fond of the blue jays and spent hours watching them.

Earlier that day Dennis had put a piece of ginger with the peanuts on the feeding platform in the backyard and had noticed the blue jays' strange reaction to it. One bird had picked the piece of the ginger up then dropped it as if it were a hot pebble. The bird then swooped to the ground where the ginger had fallen. Its feathers were puffed out and the tuft on its head was raised. It was very agitated. Its mate joined in the ruckus as they flitted around the piece of ginger and took turns pecking at it.

Dennis, thinking that was funny, had added a few more

pieces to the peanuts on the feeding platform. He wanted the feathered performance to continue and so it did. The birds were beside themselves and swooped down onto the feeder attacking each piece of ginger root until they were now all on the ground. They were so upset that they totally ignored the peanuts that they were so very fond of.

Grandma stepped onto the sun deck from the back door of the house and, deeply fascinated, watched the birds at their antics. A smile lit up her face as the blue jays let go of the last two pieces of ginger, then swooped down after them. A defiant peck on the last piece that fell seemed to satisfy the birds that the thing was now truly dead. They flew off over the trees and beyond her field of vision.

As she leaned against the railing of the sun deck just below Dennis' bedroom window, she could still hear them squawking in the distance. She was unaware that he was in his room.

As she looked in the direction where the birds had flown, she became aware of a shadow just behind to her left, and felt a subtle breeze against her neck.

Grandma hit out with sudden force and her swinging arm connected with the bird that hovered by her left shoulder. It fell lifeless at her feet. Two of its dislodged feathers floated in the warm summer breeze. She did not remember having seen that bird at the feeder before, yet it somehow looked familiar. Its milk-white wings were partly folded as if it were about to take off, but the lifeless eyes stared at her unblinking.

Grandma felt a terrible sensation in her head and her heart beat wildly in her chest. She held onto the railing of the sun deck for support and screamed. That was when she heard the soft giggle coming from the window above.

"What's the matter, Grandma?" Dennis asked, putting his head out the window as far as he could and pretending to be sympathetic. Grandma did not answer. She reached down to pick up her upper denture that had slipped out of her mouth when she screamed. As she did so, she noticed for the first time the piece of string lying beside the bird. One end was tied around its neck. Then she remembered. It was an artificial bird that had sat on one of the branches of the Christmas tree last year.

She had almost had a stroke when she discovered it hovering near her shoulder and had felt guilty when she thought she had killed it. And it turned out to be only the prank of a wicked little boy!

She wiped the denture off on her skirt and slipped it back into her mouth, then walked slowly to the door and into the house. Dennis looked through the crack in his door and saw her climb the stairs slowly and painfully. Her head was bowed and shoulders drooped. There was a sad look on her face. She looked very old and tired, very sad and alone. She passed his door without looking at it, entered her bedroom and closed the door.

Dennis backed away from his door and sat on the edge of his bed. All of a sudden he did not feel so good. He felt a sense of shame and remorse. He remembered the first day Grandma had come to live with his family. She wasn't like anybody's grandma that he knew. She never laughed at his jokes, nor did she think it was funny when he had put the frog in her shoe. She had been wild with anger when she found his toy worm in her salad. He had thought it was funny, but he discovered that Grandma had no sense of humour.

It had ended up with him being sentenced to a week without television and an open apology to her. That had been the worse part of the punishment, having to apologize. It was then that he was sure that he hated her. She had squealed on him many times since then, and grandmas weren't supposed to do that. They were supposed to be their grandsons' secret sharers, their pals and comforters. Weren't they? But with Grandma there was none of that. There was no gesture of love, and he wanted her to love him like his friend Andrew's grandma loved Andrew. He wanted her to be his friend, but she was cold and uncaring. It was obvious that she did not like him at all, so he declared war against her.

He teased her when his parents were not around. He made silly sounds to annoy her, which they did. Then she would complain to his parents and he would be duly punished. It became a vicious circle, until eventually an unspoken truce was declared and Dennis avoided Grandma as much as possible, except on rare occasions like today, when he just could not resist the temptation of playing the trick on her. Although he had gotten a good chuckle out of it, he now felt badly about it. He decided to go over and tell her he was sorry.

Dennis knocked gingerly on the closed door. There was no answer. He knocked again, a little louder this time feeling a bit braver.

"Grandma?" he said hesitantly, "are you in there? Can I come in and talk to you?"

"Talk to me about what?" her voice sounded muffled through the closed door.

"Grandma, I ..."

"I am nobody's grandma," she said in solemn resignation. Dennis was surprised. He had never heard her sound like that before. It caused him pain to think that he was the cause of her sadness.

"You are my grandmother, aren't you? Mom says so!"

"But do you say so, Dennis?" It was the first time she had called him by name in months, at least that he knew of. "Do you?" The voice behind the door insisted.

"Of course you are, Grandma! See? I call you Grandma, don't I? I play with you, don't I? But you're always telling Mom tales about me. I don't think you like me at all." He stopped to catch his breath. The feeling he now experienced made him excited and there was warmth inside. It was a feeling he had never had for Grandma before and he liked it.

"Well, do you, Grandma?" he asked, resting his palms against the door as if to feel her response through the solid wood. The door opened suddenly and Grandma stood looking down at him. She had regained her composure, but her eyes looked moist and puffy through her thick horn-rimmed glasses.

She's been crying, he thought, *and all because of me being nasty to her.*

Sadness filled his heart and overflowed. He threw himself into her arms and sobbed "I am sorry. Grandma. I won't play anymore tricks on you again, ever! I want us to be friends, like Andrew and his grandma are! She bakes him cookies every Friday, you know?"

Doris Smith hugged her grandson to her gently. This curly-headed pint-sized who had caused her such consternation in the two years she had lived with him, was indeed her beloved daughter's child, her flesh and blood. Her daughter and son-in-law had been very good to her in every way. She suddenly realized that she had been missing out on the wonderful relationship all grandparents should have with their grandchildren. A relationship which, through selfishness and anger, she had denied herself and Dennis. She had one grandchild and resolved from now on to enjoy him, frogs and all.

Debbie Lund could not believe her eyes when she walked in through the front door and stood in the hallway. Her widowed mother was stroking her ten-year-old son's head as she held him close to her. It was something she had never thought would happen and she was very pleased and relieved. She remembered feeling a bit apprehensive about inviting her mother to come and live with them after her father died. She had hoped that, being with them, her mother would be able to cope better with her husband's tragic death and be more open with her feelings.

Doris Smith had never been an outgoing person and had never openly showed affection, even when she was a child. Debbie remembered always going to her father whenever she needed comfort or reassurance. Her mother was a good housewife who cared very much for her family, but because of her own strict upbringing was unable or reluctant to show her feelings for someone she loved. Not until she was in college did she realize the truth about her mother, and, with understanding on her part, their relationship had improved. They had become more like friends than mother and daughter. Now, in her adulthood, Debbie was closer to her mother than she was when a child.

After her husband accidentally drowned on a fishing trip, Doris had sunk into a deep depression. Coming to live with Debbie and her family had proved helpful in relieving the condition. She seemed happier and enjoyed the company of her daughter and son-in-law. Although Doris did not show it, Debbie knew from experience that she was fond of her grandson.

Dennis, however, was used to love and affection being shown openly around him. His mother had vowed when she was a teenager that her children would never have to wonder if they were loved — they would be told and shown as often as possible — and she had kept her word.

Grandma did not live up to Dennis' expectations and it had left him disappointed and angry. The situation in the Lund household was becoming strained and Debbie and her husband Bert had recently played with the idea of getting Grandma into a seniors' apartment. They firmly believed, however, that the extended family setting would benefit all in the long run, and had decided to put this idea on hold, hoping that their son would very soon get over his disappointment and learn to accept Grandma as she was.

And now her prayers were answered. Her mother was hugging her child — something she had never done with her. At last they had ironed out their differences. It had taken two years, but it had happened.

A few hours later while getting ready for his baseball game, Dennis called down to his mother to inquire where his uniform was. He had found his T-shirt, but not the pants. His grandmother answered instead.

"I heard you telling your mother that the pants were too long, so I hemmed them up for you." Grandma had a strange smile on her face. "You'll find them on my bed, Dennis." The smile lingered knowingly, but went unnoticed by her daughter, who was busy washing carrots at the kitchen sink.

Minutes went by before Dennis descended the stairs and presented himself in the kitchen before the two women.

"Look Mom!" he said, but his stare was fixed on his grandmother. They looked at him for a moment and fought back the urge to laugh. Dennis was ready for his baseball game dressed in his team uniform. The right pant leg was ankle length and the left one about an inch below the knee. Debbie looked at her mother, who appeared completely unaware of what was going on in the kitchen at that moment.

"Do you want to change the pants, honey?" she asked, still stifling the desire to laugh.

"Nah!" Dennis answered loud enough for Grandma to hear. He smiled resignedly and adjusted the cap on his head. "Grandma might feel badly that she can't sew." With that, he picked up his bat and mitt from the floor and walked out the door.

INNER TURMOIL

*T*he scorching rays of the July sun engulfed the lonely beach like an industrial oven at its peak of operation. It sent the four of us rushing back into the cool, refreshing sea for temporary relief.

I held Precious in my arms as I entered the softly rolling waves. I laid her on my stomach as I back-floated parallel to the beach.

"You look like a sea otter carrying its offspring," my wife Silvie offered. She was closer to the shore, doing the jellyfish float and allowing the soft waves to gently crash over her. "Get her in the water before she gets her back burnt." "Pearlie," she shouted, standing now and looking past me. "How far are you going? You might get a cramp out there and get into trouble!"

I looked out to sea and saw Pearlie swimming out to Sandy Cove, a small island nearby. She was using her arms and legs. She was a much stronger swimmer than Silvie was and usually ventured further. I ladled water simultaneously with both hands over my daughter's back, with no response. She usually giggles loudly and returns the favour.

I raised my head a bit to look at her face and found that she was falling asleep. I raised myself out of the water, holding her above the waves, and walked towards shore. Silvie stood up as I approached her. Ringlets of her black hair that had escaped the confinement of her bathing cap clung to her forehead and cheeks.

"What's the matter? What's wrong?" I looked back and saw Pearlie swimming back to shore. She must have thought something was wrong with my exit from the water. "Is the baby all right?" she asked, as she walked towards us.

"She is sleeping!" Silvie and I said simultaneously.

We walked quickly to the spreading almond tree where we had left our picnic basket and blanket. My wife unfolded the blanket, then placed our baby's padded blanket on the middle. I put Precious down on her stomach and lay down beside her so that my arm cradled her head. The women sat down and began handing out sandwiches.

"This is nice," Pearlie said as she handed Silvie and me each a bottle of frosty Ting, and replaced the lid of the small igloo cooler we had given her two years before when she had visited us in Hamilton.

"What is?" Silvie asked after downing half the contents of her bottle. "What is what?" Pearlie looked at Silvie, then at me, then back at Silvie. "You said 'this is nice,' and I wanted to know what 'this' is!"

I was just about to say something explanatory when I realized that they were bantering each other, as they were wont to do whenever the occasion arises. It used to bug me a lot at first, this unnecessary stretching of a simple question or statement, pulling it back and forth for minutes until they dissolved into laughter. I have gotten used to it by now, and usually tune them out completely until the situation was resolved.

"I was saying that having you guys here on holiday is nice. Just relaxing on this nice beach, soaking up the sun and the sea, and enjoying your company, is more than nice. It's downright fun! You know." Silvie was about to say something but changed her mind as our friend continued in contemplative tones. "I haven't had a holiday in nearly two years and it was beginning to tell on me."

"Yes, you're two years older and look it," I jokingly interjected and everyone laughed. Precious lifted her head, eyes still closed, and set it back down with her face away from us.

"No, all joking aside," Pearlie continued, "I haven't felt so relaxed and happy for a long time."

"It has been a relaxing holiday for us, too," I offered, tossing my empty Ting bottle on the sand near the basket. Pearlie stretched over and picked it up and leaned it against the tree beside her. Then I remembered that she saved up empty pop bottles for the 'bottle man' who collected them every month.

"Sorry," I said, and meant it.

"I know that you Canadians don't give much thought to simple things like a couple of soft drink bottles worth a few cents, but ..."

"Now you're going to get her started on her pet peeve about the rich Canadians and the 'poor' Jamaicans," Silvie said jumping up and throwing off her towel, which landed in a heap on the blanket at my feet. "I'm going back for a swim. This heat is forcing me to. I'll make it quick and come back to relieve you, Sam." She touched my forehead fleetingly and sauntered off towards the water.

"Wait for me." Pearlie jumped up and ran past her friend into the water. They began splashing each other, laughing as they did. I lowered myself onto the blanket beside my daughter, draping her protectively with my body. This beautiful sleeping angel was my child, I mused. My darling Silvie's and mine. Her name was Claudine Monique McKay.

When she was three months pregnant, Silvie had started to bleed and threatened to miscarry. She had been admitted to hospital on complete bed rest for a month in an effort to save this pregnancy. She had miscarried our first and second at two and two and a half months respectively, so everyone was concerned that she carry this child safely to term.

Our baby girl was delivered at thirty-two weeks' gestation, all four-and-a-half pounds of her. We had finally hit the jackpot after ten years of marriage and two disappointments. At last we had a precious bundle that was a part of us. We nicknamed her "Precious."

I thought of how much closer we had become since the beginning of this vacation. Neither of us had visited Jamaica for eight years. There had been a wave of political unrest that had plagued the country. There had been wanton shootings of people in Kingston and the suburbs, as well as in rural areas which had affected the county's tourist trade. Now the country and tourism were beginning to get back to normal.

Pearlie and Silvie were now sitting at the water's edge with their legs being washed by the soft waves. Pearlie was relating a story about a man they had found asleep in the front yard of the Health Clinic where she worked. He was lying on his back in the hot sun stark naked. His erect penis was draped with his only piece of clothing — a dirty red cloth cap. They were laughing almost into a state of hysterics.

I smiled and said out loud, "You'd think they would have

seen enough naked men in their nursing profession to prevent them getting hysterical over one who decides to use his organ as a hat rack." They laughed harder and my wife dropped to her knees in mirth.

Suddenly there was a strong whiff of smoke in the air. I recognized the pungent odour that clung to my nostrils. "Ganja!" I said softly to myself. "Somebody nearby is smoking ganja!" I had never seen the stuff but would recognize its smell anywhere.

⌒

I was ten years old that summer when I had gone mango gathering with my nine-year-old cousin, Myles, and my seven-year-old sister, Terri. We had wandered over hills and vales, climbing trees, checking out birds' nests and eating mangoes along the way. We suddenly came upon a tin shack on the side of a hill and readily crept closer to investigate.

A voice boomed out in perfect schoolroom English from above us. "What are you three children doing up here by yourself?" We stopped, frozen in our tracks. We looked up into the kind eyes and rustic, bearded face of a Rastafarian who was sitting on the bent trunk of a coconut tree above where we were standing. His thick, matted, black hair hung around his brown face and down to his shoulders. He wore a clean, loosely fitted sleeveless shirt over khaki shorts. A matchstick moved rhythmically in the right side of his moustached lips. He was the first Rasta I had ever seen close up and I eyed him suspiciously.

He seemed to sense our uneasiness and in a kind voice said, "No need to be afraid. You'll be okay!" He said his name was Founder and was using the hut as a retreat — a place to meditate.

I secretly visited Founder as often as I could for the next three weeks of that summer and learned a lot about the trees and forest, the birds and insects, life and its mysteries from him. He told me of the need to embrace peace and love. That there are two kinds of Rastas. The authentic ones were peaceful, loving and helpful to their fellow men. They took pride in their personal hygiene and surroundings. Never used ganja except for medicinal purposes and lived in hope of going back to their homeland in Africa (they believe that Ethiopia is their homeland and Haile

Selassie their king). The false Rastas, he said were dirty and vio-
lent people who would not work except for cultivating, smoking
and trafficking in ganja. Then one day after an absence of about
two weeks, I had gone back up the hill to Founder's hut and
found that it was no more.

It had been a beautiful Sunday morning, as Jamaican
Sundays usually are. I was awakened by a commotion in the
street close to our home. I ran through the open door that joined
my sister's room with mine and looked through her window that
faced Drawstring Hill. Terri was still asleep with her Black
Mambo doll lying beside her.

I could see smoke billowing in the sky over the area where I
knew Founder's hut was located. People were coming out of
their houses to watch the smoke across the hill, while others ran
towards it. I used a short cut that took me to the scene in no time
at all. The place was teeming with onlookers and there was a jeep
with the Jamaican Defense insignia on its hood, parked across the
footpath that led up to the hill.

There were also two police cars on the road below the hill. A
soldier was walking two handcuffed Rastas towards the road.
Two finely dressed men in suits and ties were led down the hill
next. Then the bottom of the bucket fell out for me, for coming
down next, being pushed and prodded by the policemen, and
shouting profanities at his captors, was Founder. His hair, face,
and clothes were dirty and his feet wore sandals made from rub-
ber tire strips. His hands were handcuffed behind him and he
walked with a staggering gait.

A soldier with a rifle slung over his shoulder walked in
front to clear the way, as people had begun to crowd the path to
get a better look. When they got close to the tree stump on which
I was standing, I shouted his name in confused dismay. He
stopped and our eyes met for a fraction of a second before he was
pushed forward by the soldier. He had fallen onto his face and
was yanked back on his feet by two policemen bringing up the
rear.

I was in shock. This was not the Founder I had come to
know and respect. The one who had explained to me that the Red
Sea in not really red, that it was the reflection from the red soil on
its bed. He looked like a wild animal. His dazed-looking beady

red eyes protruded from a haggard face, and his clothes were very dirty. He had a cut below his right eye that started bleeding freely when he fell.

The officers appeared not to have noticed this bleeding and continued to push him down the hill towards the waiting vehicles.

I was heartbroken. I sat on the tree stump, dazed and watched as the vehicles drove away. Then all was quiet until "What are you doing up here son? You should go home!" I looked up into the face of one of the officers who had stayed behind to continue to burn the tall plants that were still untouched by the fire.

"What did Founder do?" I asked in a dry raspy voice.

"You know him?" the man had asked. Then, with concern suddenly showing on his face, and before I could answer his question, he threw another one at me.

"Did he ever give you ganja to smoke, son? Did he?"

"What's ganja?" I had asked, then, "No, I don't smoke. He doesn't smoke either. He is ..." The officer looked relieved. "He was a wanted criminal, son. Cultivates and sells the weed to people as far away as Kingston. We raided the place on a tip and burned his crop. He attacked and badly injured one of the officers before he was subdued. You should have nothing to do with Rastas, son. Now go on home."

I looked at the smouldering rubble on the deserted hill and tears welled up in my eyes. I ran home sobbing, blinded with sorrow and disappointment. Founder had been my friend, my teacher — a father figure. I guess I had tried to see my father through his eyes. Now it was all over. Founder had lied to me, disappointed and abandoned me, just as my own father had done when I was four years old. I had lived with the disappointment and distrust, hiding the details from my mother to this day.

I had often wondered what became of him in the end. Did he manage somehow to go to Ethiopia and see his king? Or was he doing hard labour in prison? I was suddenly wrenched out of my reverie by the sound of gunshots. Two were fired in quick succession, in the nearness of the forest fringing the beach. We were all startled and looked in unison towards where the sound came from. Two pea-doves flew out of the woods above our heads and out of sight. Trying to sound calm, I stated that someone might be bird hunting. I thought of the times when I was young and went bird hunting with my uncle. Nonetheless I felt anxious and afraid. I was afraid for the safety of my family and our friend.

We were in a very isolated area and our car was parked on the road a good way from where we were. I suggested that we start back to the car since it was getting hotter and the heat might affect the baby adversely. They readily agreed.

We quickly gathered up the blanket, picnic bag, and cooler. The women donned their beach coats and hats and I put Precious' T-shirt and sunbonnet on her. I decided to carry Precious so that we could move faster.

As soon as I picked her up, the baby was fast asleep and drooling on my neck. I shifted her to my other shoulder and the towel that covered her fell to the ground. As I stooped to pick it up I became aware that we were no longer alone on the beach. Two men were walking towards us.

One was short and stocky, perhaps in his fifties. He was light-skinned, with curly, greying black hair and beard. His faded blue jeans were cut off at the ankle and his sockless feet wore brown loafers. His short-sleeved white shirt was unbuttoned and billowed in the wind. The other man was Rastafarian, the dirty, unkempt kind that Founder had talked about so many childhood years ago. His unseen hair was piled under a knitted tubular black cap that looked like a termite mound and his beard was coir-red and matted. He wore a pair of brown trousers and a black shirt. He was barefooted and carried a large machete in his right hand and a half-empty pop bottle in the other.

The women must have seen them at the same time as I did. They stopped and waited for me to catch up. I could sense their fear and mine became magnified. My heart pounded wildly in my chest much like it did when I was a child and saw a Rasta, after the Founder incident. A million thoughts milled about in my head. Could these be the men responsible for the gunshot sounds we heard a few minutes ago? Was my family's life at risk? What if they attacked us? Would I be able to defend the women and myself? I only had a camping knife that I carried in the waist of my swim trunks.

Horrible scenes were being conjured in my mind. I saw my wife and our friend being brutally raped and hacked to death with Ras' machete, right before my eyes. I saw them rape my baby daughter and throw her lifeless body into the sea. And all I could do was jab wildly at the air with my camping knife while I slowly died of gunshot wounds in my failed efforts to save my family. I could see the headlines in the newspaper back home — *Vacationers Murdered on Lonely Beach in Jamaica. Husband helpless to Defend Family.*

"Let me carry the baby now, Sam. You must be tired now carrying her." Silvie's voice broke into my thoughts like a gush of cold air into a stuffy room. She came towards me with open arms and a noncommittal face.

Smart girl, my wife, I thought. With her holding the baby I would be free to concentrate on the 'enemies,' with a better chance of defense if necessary. After all, it was my duty, my obligation to protect my family. Seems it has always been my obligation to protect someone.

Being the older of two children and my father deserting us when I was four, the task of protector was thrust upon me and I have always felt it was my duty to comply, even now that we are adults and have families of our own. In fact it has even been a bone of contention between me and my wife, who frequently accused me of being more attentive and protective of my relatives than of my own wife and child. Her accusations always hurt me deeply because I knew that they weren't true. Were they?

Now it seemed she was challenging me again with those thirteen words and her gesture to protect my family from harm.

I was scared as hell and maybe showed it. I looked at my wife, who was now holding the baby close to her, and I felt like the lucky man that I was. I noticed that Pearlie had Precious' feeding bottle still full of apple juice. She had tied one end of her scarf firmly around its neck, and the other end twisted around her hand. What in hell's name was she doing that for? I thought. She stood up and gently swung the glass bottle from her right hand, while gripping the picnic bag in her left.

And then I knew. It would be a clubbing tool if needs be.

I looked at my wife and our friend. How wonderful it was to have people like them around me! It makes one feel brave even if he is not. I smiled a lingering smile at them, then looked up into the smiling faces of Ras and his friend.

"Iry, Master!" Ras said, swinging his machete slightly at his side and flashing an approving smile at us. "You been taking a sea bath, man! Nice!" His lingering smile revealed incisors brown stained maybe from long use of smoking, poor oral hygiene, or both.

I was standing between Pearlie and the men (Silvie had moved off, saying she had to take the baby out of the sun). Using my best Jamaican patois, I said "Yes, the sea-water mek her tired an' sleepy."

"Yu don' want her fe get sun stroke, an' dis is jus' de kinda day fe do dat." Ras' pal interjected.

"Yu know it man," I replied in a forced calm voice. The two men started walking away. "Tek care a' yu nice family, Bredda Man," Ras said, "Dem precious."

"Peace!" offered his friend as they quickened their steps away from us. I gazed at their backs as they disappeared around a bend.

I looked towards my wife and found that our friend had caught up to her and they were now close to where we had parked the car. I breathed a sigh of relief and ran across the sandy beach to catch up with the women, for although I was relieved about the good encounter, I could not put the sound of the gunshots out of my mind. I thought that the sooner we left this place, the better it would be for us.

I caught up with the women just as they arrived at the car. We all tumbled into the vehicle, each saying aloud how thankful we were to be safely off that beach.

A reflective silence settled over the four of us as we departed from that place. Precious continued in sleep on Pearlie's lap, oblivious of what the adults had just been through. Both Silvie and Pearlie had their eyes closed, though I am not sure if they were asleep.

I thought of the encounter on the beach and the unresolved turmoil in my mind resulting from those encounters back on Drawstring Hill when I was ten years old. I told myself that I would go back there again soon, in order to find some closure. To face the ghosts of the past, in order to resolve my inner turmoil of the present.

For Poetry's Sake

Untitled

It's spring, and I feel young again,
And light and warm and happy;
Ready to throw off winter's strain,
See how my steps are snappy?
Likewise, my mind feels free,
That's what spring does to me.

Tomorrow's Dreams, Today

My lofty thoughts and far-off dreams
Of what tomorrow might be
Can stifle and snuff out the beams
Of light, so my eyes won't see.
I cannot afford my life to waste
While I for tomorrow pray.
If I must dream, I'll dream in haste,
Live tomorrow's dream today.

All my tomorrows gathered in
This moment I hold so dear.
Future desires and hopes within
Me must blossom now, it's clear.
I may not see tomorrow, though;
Darkness may blot out the way,
I have to travel the path I know,
And I must do it today.

The world is changing, and I know
Change is expected of me,
I would that I could live and grow
Into tomorrow and be
Able to plan a future rare,
Love, joy and peace all the way,
But I can't. So with urgent care
I will live tomorrow's dream today.

My Long-Forgotten Dream

Oh, I see myself as I was thirty years ago or more,
Then, the flower of youth and beauty few have ever known before.
Then the golden dawn of daylight blossomed full upon my lips;
Now, the cold, dark night of autumn swells the flesh around my hips.

And the eyes that once shone bright within my world, like stars above,
Are cataract-cloudy now, nor even can glimpse the light of love.
And the legs that leaped across the playgrounds, climbed many
                                                    stout trees,
Are now harbingers of bunions, chasing only memories.

But I close my eyes and drift off in a world of yesteryears,
Where in youth my joys were many and had far surpassed my tears.
And the laughter which resounded through the hills and glens was mine.
As a child so free from cares and fears, I was allowed to shine.

But as time moved on and I grew older, things changed for the worse.
All the weight of age, responsibilities became a curse.
For the fret of care, my countenance, my lucid eyes have dulled,
And the vibrant beating of a heart in love today is lulled.

Though I now look back through days gone by with laments or a sigh,
My past has enhanced my present, over spilled milk I dare not cry.
Today is mine regardless, I must stifle my frightened screams,
And just be content with dusting off my long-forgotten dreams.

The Might of Dreams

As the daylight seconds blossom and bloom
Fully into midnight flowers,
My drowsy and sluggish thoughts all make room
For dreams, in my sleeping hours.
Events hidden from sane and conscious thought,
Or those forced to be restrained,
Take over, unhindered, unchecked, unsought,
When they are no longer chained.

A disembodied spirit, I would fly
In the darkness of my dreams
To far-away places, roofed by the sky,
And lit by bright moonbeams.
Or be thrown into dismal dungeons by foes,
Captured by some warring tribe.
Conquer Everest, secret spies expose,
Be a dancer or a scribe.

In the unconsciousness of dream, I can
Do the strangest things. I see
Myself in strange roles, not a conscious plan
Would allow me so to be.
Thus the might of dreams can most things overpower,
And most things accomplish too.
Would that my good dreams could blossom and flower,
And make all of them come true.

Tomorrow

Tomorrow,
One more chance of life to live.
Like water seeping through the sun-parched earth,
                    unchecked and free,
Seeing tomorrow revitalizes me.
In its time frame, the actions, words, and thoughts
Emitted by such as I, lucky enough
To see once more tomorrow as it dawns upon my sight,
Encourages me to fully submit
Myself to all its ebbs and flows.
It knows my destiny,
I know my ignorance.
But I'll live life even as tomorrow's sun is lost to view.

Tomorrow,
Oh, for a precious day,
As it breaks forth from its bastion prison of mystery,
And bathed in golden glows of a high sun.
And maybe fanned by gentle wafting winds.
Tomorrow is a newborn, emerging in innocence,
Untainted, not yet fouled by over-spills
From yesterday's dark pains and screaming sorrows
Until I make it so.
But oh, all would be lost
Should all my tomorrows be just mirrors of today!

How Time Flies!

Spring came and went before we knew it,
Time is moving on in haste.
And summer, we will soon be through it,
Time has no time to waste.
Time moves on, never lies
Around to hear the cries
Of stragglers in its way,
Time flies on night and day.

It waits for no one, not a moment
Will Time give up for aught.
If foolishly it is lost and spent,
Time just cannot be caught.
It is fickle, selfish too,
And does what it must do.
Moves on, ignores the cries
Of 'Heaven, how time flies!'

Time races on through seasoned hours
Toward infinity,
While mortals stop to smell the flowers
Of life, and reality.
Our weary souls must pause
Along the way, because
With Time we cannot race;
Time flies to keep the pace.

Echoes From the Past

Oh, they call and call so sweetly
From across the silent past,
And enfold my heart completely
As they hug and hold me fast.
Memories of youth and laughter,
Joyful sounds from distant years,
Echo silently, long after
They fill up my heart and ears.

Silently resound and warn me,
With such feelings I can't lose.
Echoes from the past induce me
With longings I have to choose.
For only the joyful moments
I'm remembering at will,
As they swirl like gentle torrents,
And my eager mind would fill.

Echoes from the past resounding,
Gently touch my mind before
Vanishing, with speed astounding,
To oblivion once more.
So when pleasant memories find me
Musing over times gone by,
Hopefully they will remind me
To enjoy life ere I die.

Contemplating Time

How the years fly by real fast,
When we take stock of the past.
Time that seems sometimes to go
In our thinking, mostly slow,
Has been racing, moving on,
And before we know, it's gone,
Leaving us to wonder why
We stood still while time raced by.

Days of yore when fledgling hearts,
Light and lively, kept the parts
Of each body well composed.
Concentrating only on
Joys and pleasures, ere they are gone.
And those days were meant to be
Spent in leisure, from cares free.

Contemplating times gone by
May incur in us a sigh
For the loss of carefree days,
And the parting of the ways
Of our childhood's noble schemes,
And those far-fetched unfilled dreams
Which were left behind, but still
Keep the memories with us still.

Carefree Days Lost

As I alighted from the bus and skirted yonder burn,
Then rounded a wee hill, before the corner I could turn,
I did espy
A rogue magpie.
As he flew by
Across my path, the cares of life at once my mind did spurn.

And on the hill sat a wee lad, a-whistling loud and strong,
While his black terrier chased some phantom rabbit far and long.
The echoed sound
Circled around
Till my ears found
And took possession in my mind, creating a new song.

I sat beneath a tree and listened to the young lad's trill
Which siphoned the sun-warmed air from yonder craggy hill.
The words I wrote
To match each note
The whistler's quote,
Cannot do justice to that beauteous sound, and never will.

The joy and freedom of young blood as demonstrated then
While that small lad in carefree guise charmed all on hill and glen,
Can never come back
When we've lost track,
And fervor lack,
Because no longer are we carefree boys, but worried men.

O Canada! Our Mother

A mother cannot afford to favour one child above the other,
From the oldest to the youngest,
From the weakest to the strongest,
Yes, the plain ones and the fairest,
Each nursed with your love the rarest.
Though the cries of all your children
May sound different now than back then,
Canada, to all your children be a wise and caring mother.
Love the rich ones and the poor ones,
Guide the stumbling and the sure ones,
The new-comers and the old ones,
The frightened and the bold ones,
For to them there is no other, as they all call you their mother.

Smiles on multicoloured faces reflect the love each embraces,
And we come together as one,
Knowing each is a native son
Of a country grand, resplendent,
With a love strong and evident
To all those who would behold
This land rising from the cold,
And embrace her children dear,
Each one's voice willing to hear.
Each child nourishes the other, blest by Canada our mother.
Nurturing us through smiles and tears,
Loving us through months and years,
As we always will love you, Mother of vast and varied faces.

A Special Place

Yes! This is what I now call home,
When friends and relatives all come,
Where I am counted, and then some,
A special place to be.
My Eden, where I go and come,
A special place for me.

For thirty years I've watched her grow
Into my heart, and now I know
I cannot leave, I can't let go,
Or break the bond we share.
Because I really love her so,
And for her really care.

I fell in love when first we met,
Her rugged beauty woos me yet,
And will continue to, I'll bet,
For she owns me through and through.
This love affair I can't forget,
No matter what I do.

Or where I go from Hamilton,
I'll be back where I do belong;
Though I'm just her adopted son
I'm hers, as she is mine.
My home away from home, the one
Thread that does my life entwine.

Yes, Hamilton is a special place
Where I have carved out my own space,
My obligations gladly face,
Loyal, always will be;
For she's a city charged with grace
For all her sons, and me.

Views From the Mountain

I sometimes sit for many hours near Gore Park's cool fountain,
Now I sit amidst nature's bowers and get views from the mountain.
The placid waters of the bay, its tranquil glassy stare
On a quiet day in winter, when the cold harbour lies bare.

Or as dank waves gallop to shore and seagulls scream at will,
Converging, hovering by the score, and manure freely spill.
The sun-drenched outline, steeped in gold, of the escarpment's face,
Where many stories are untold of this beautiful place.

The crowded city core that seems to kneel beneath the mount,
And glassed skyscrapers, as each gleams, now too many to count.
Looking down on the Jolly Cut and viewing its hairpin turns,
Cowering beneath outcrops of rocks that form deep baseless urns.

Toronto's skyline to the right, sometimes the Skyway Bridge,
A million neon lights at nights flush shadows from the ridge.
Floral or rock gardens that line the path to city core,
That lonely, unused rail incline, Sam Lawrence Park, and more.

The place where Easter sunrise services are held, and more;
Where everyone can scan with ease Hamilton's own lakeshore.
From any Mountain site it seems, whether day is dull or clear,
I find great themes to write about with the view I get from there.

Percé Visited

Percé, you are so beautiful
As all rustic beauty goes.
Nestled between mountain and sea,
Your living spirit glows.
Hemmed in by forest green and lush,
A wide and steep backyard,
And up front is your briny deep,
Where Percé Rock stands guard

The visitors that you attract,
Humans and birds alike,
Flock here in droves when weather is fair,
Leave ere cold weather strikes.
I'm one of those just passing through,
With a day or two to spare,
Percé, I'll long remember you,
And I'm glad I was here.

East Coast Adventure

We travelled for two weeks to the East Coast
On one of Cardinal's tours;
The vacation that I've enjoyed the most
Was on those Maritime shores.

The escort/driver team, each a traveller's friend,
Were dear Ruth and Monsieur Bob;
And from the tour's beginning to its end,
They did a fantastic job.

We were picked up in downtown Hamilton,
Joined an international group;
First names were being used, like Ed, Louis, John,
By the time we hit Rivière du Loup.

We saw Hopewell Rocks and encountered whales
At Cheticamp. Oh! That was fun.
Picturesque Cabot and Evangeline Trails
Were experiences second to none.

Got informative city tours; saw the sea,
And walked their boardwalks with ease.
Saw lots of marine birds — cormorants flying free,
And lush forests clustered with trees.

Surely I wish I could linger always,
And drink in the beauty that's there.
Relax and just bask in those soft, tranquil days,
And forget what it is like elsewhere.

Highlights? Well we crossed Confederation Bridge,
Trudged in Prince Edward Island's red dirt.
At Peggy's Cove climbed on each granite ridge,
Watched the St. John River revert.

Climbed down steel steps, saw Hopewell's sandstone rocks,
Went to Green Gables and Woodleigh.
For Atlantic Time, forward went the clocks,
Saw apple orchards in Grand Pré.

There were mudflats at low tide in riverbeds,
Lily ponds with live frogs and toads.
Sightings of seals; I saw only their heads;
And narrow, hilly, winding roads.

I have experienced the East Coast on this tour,
I have seen its green hillsides, its seas.
Marine life, especially birds by the score.
With the slow pace, I felt at ease.

Foods like fresh fish, lobster, and clam chowder too,
Blueberries and blueberry pies.
Saltwater taffy and dulse that you chew,
Though different, I gave them good tries.

To the East Coast again I would like to go,
Because the sea is in my blood;
And Prince Edward Island earth's bright red glow
Is like Jamaica's bauxite mud …

… So I just felt quite at home while out there;
Maybe even my home I would move it.
Did I have fun in the Atlantic air?
Well, I have videos to prove it!

Whale Watching in Cheticamp

Whale watching in the Atlantic
Off Nova Scotia's coast,
Was the highlight of my holidays,
And what I'll remember most.

The sun hung low in clear blue sky,
Tinting the soft waves gold.
And the red-green hills towering on high
Were rare beauties to behold!

Aboard the Seaside Cruise 'Love Boat,'
Whale watching I did go
With twenty other 'Cardinals,'
All primed to view the show.
And what a show it was! The whales
Surrounded the 'Love Boat,'
The minkes and the pilot whales,
With baby whales afloat.

They watched us watch them cruise and play,
Show off smooth glistening mounds.
I'll not forget the gentle way they glide,
Nor yet the sounds
They made as they sliced the air
With grace, they showed no fear.
I'll long remember this event,
Even when I'm old and grey,
Of whale watching at Cheticamp
On that memorable day.

The Little-Leaguers

They swing their bats and kick the balls,
Can move the pucks with speed.
As quarterbacks, they tackle well,
Score touchdowns their teams need.
They move the ball across the court,
Gain baskets with much ease,
And those who prefer track and field,
Will team up as they please.

These little-leaguers practise well,
And most master their game.
With patience, each one hones his skill
And dreams of future fame
Of playing with the Tiger Cats,
The Raptors or Blue Jays;
Of being another Wayne Gretzsky
And knowing fame always.

It is a long road to the top,
And it takes hard work, true grit,
Parental encouragement,
And athletes who refuse to quit,
Coaches who dedicate their time,
Venues for practising,
The chance each child needs in his sport
To really do his thing.

Each city little-leaguer
Who has pro sports on his mind
Finds inspiration close at hand,
The best that he can find.
If his ambition is to be
Professional someday,
Then with hard work, patience, and luck,
He'll make it all the way.

A Bird-Watching Weekend

We traveled from Wesley Chapel on a warm October day,
Three carloads of bird-watching novices, with lots to say
And lots to sing about,
In joyous voices shout,
As we travelled west to Kingsville, on the 401 highway.

We finally arrived that afternoon at ten to four,
After stopping once to eat and righting each unplanned detour.
We gazed in utmost awe,
Marvelled at what we saw,
Especially the geese, which to me, were the central core.

The 'air show' was spectacular; oh boy, they hate that truck!
And I was fascinated with the colours of each duck.
We all were lost for words,
The beauty of the birds
Made me acknowledge that my blessings are much more than luck.

We left Jack Miner's Bird Sanctuary well satisfied;
We'd toured the museum, the grounds, and a lone swan we spied.
Sat in the stadium
Behind Jack Miner's home,
And read about his life and work from his birth until he died.

The couples all paired up in double bedrooms for the night,
After locating our motel, which somehow was a plight.
Singles were left to share;
We didn't really care
Except for times when sleepers' snores would put the geese to flight.

Colosantis Gardens was the next place on the list,
Its flowers and shrubs and animals, craft wares and straw to twist.
The petting zoo that smells,
A place to eat as well,
The basket weaver and those orange trees I almost missed.

Then we were off to Point Pelee, Canada's southmost shore,
Took in the boardwalk through the marsh, saw catfish by the score.
The observation post,
Scanning the marshy coast,
Then hopping on the train to Pelee Point and our last tour.

It was indeed a trip that I will treasure all my life,
And thanks is due to organizer Gillman and his wife,
To Frank and Allan Lahl,
The drivers, and to all
Who travelled down to Kingsville on a weekend free from strife.

It was a trip that sure enriched my spirit, as my mind,
For to the plight of the world's wildlife I cannot be blind.
What good I can, I'll do
For they're God's creatures too,
And to the least of these I am commissioned to be kind.

The Bird-Girl

She sat by the window and watched them fly by,
Eyes glued to the sky.
Without knowing why,
The little girl had a compulsion to fly,
Up, up and beyond the blue.

The doves softly cooed as they perched on the tree
Where Jasmine could see
Them happy and free.
If she couldn't walk, then it would most likely be
That like the birds, she could fly too.

She pulled herself forward and hung from the ledge
Above the rose hedge,
Her life on the edge.
And then as she let go, freedom was a pledge
That wonderfully came true.

She soared off at once with the birds at her side,
She circled with pride,
Not knowing she'd died.
Her body, which her mom held close, as she cried,
Was lifeless and limp and blue.

She was now a bird flying higher and free,
At last she could see
All the world, and now she,
The bird-girl, could fly over land, over sea,
And pain she no longer knew.

Somebody's Mother

A thud is heard beside the rubbish heap
Behind the corner store
Where cold winds linger and ghostly shadows creep.
This sound cuts to the core.
A voice whispers in forced and measured spurts,
Words I can barely hear.
It sputters out in agony "It hurts!"
Urgently, I draw near.

She looks quite old and bent, so poorly clad,
She has lived from hand to mouth.
Malnourished, bruised, unwashed, rejected, sad,
Frightened, on her way out.
Her dying place — a freezing concrete wall
Against which rests her head;
And by her side a tattered bundle small.
Old newspaper is her bed.

Her callused hands and feet, her windburnt face,
Torn scarf could not protect.
And puffy eyelids, chapped lips, each a trace
Of long, severe neglect.
I see her in my mind somewhere, ill-used,
Of dignity deprived.
Left starving for affection, being abused,
As a derelict she thrived.

Wanders the cities' streets, alleys, out-backs,
Scrounges for food to eat.
Her sole possessions tote in paper sacks;
Hot meals are a rare treat.
Sleeps below the skies, whether it snows or rains.
On the fringes of life live.
Dubbed a 'bag lady' and as such remains
With naught but love to give …

And none to give it to, this lone outcast;
Not a soul to call friend.
Alone in death's throes she reflects on the past,
As her life nears its end.
"I am your friend," I whisper in her ear,
"And you are not alone,
Help is on the way, you'll be all right, don't fear."
I feel chilled to the bone.

A small crowd gathers, no one she would know,
While in this dying state.
Some stare, some look away, some murmur low,
Looks of pity, of hate.
I hold her close and try to share my coat,
Her shivering frame to warm,
As icy winds around us loudly gloat
I'm filled with new alarm.

But she is well beyond being harmed, I know
And hope her spirit will
Enjoy some sense of peace, lost long ago,
Her fading life to fill.
I hug her. Her eyes light up with a smile,
Her lips contort to speak.
I think, that ambulance has been called a while,
She is getting very weak.

She says, "The stars are bright tonight and low,
That big one there is mine.
It's sent to light the way that I must go,
And for me it does shine.
I was somebody's mother once," says she,
"Loved, as you perhaps are."
With that she smiles again and looks at me,
Then leaves to claim her star.

Street Dwellers

A profligate lifestyle desired,
Often by circumstance is willed;
They are reduced to such low estate,
Their lives with emptiness are filled.
They roam aimlessly the back alleys,
Frequent the bus stations and malls;
With diligent ease search through garbage,
Bed down 'neath the stars when night falls.

They endure this tragic existence,
Accept everything fate will give;
Posessionless, friendless, and clueless,
They all die before they can live.
Distant from society's morals,
On the fringe of uncertainty dwell;
Till the flickering light is snuffed out,
And each soul leaves its living hell.

Let the Blow Fall

Let the blow fall, I expect it,
The inevitable hour;
Let it fall, I can't reject it
Or its final power.
I was born for such a moment
While in this world I linger;
And when borrowed time is all spent,
And I'm hooked in death's finger,
I must then relinquish gladly
To the silent reaper
What was loaned; though perhaps sadly,
As I'm sinking deeper.

Let the blow fall now, tomorrow,
Next year, when it pleases.
I'm held hostage to its horror
As it smirks and teases.
Life's knife handle is in its keeping,
I, the blade am holding;
Held captive, waking or sleeping,
Need I bother scolding?
I will live life and not languish,
Nor shall I be clinging
To gloom. If I have my last wish,
I will go out singing.

Poor Man, Rich Man

His modest mansion is a thatched-roof shack,
In a garden of flowers growing wild.
His wardrobe is the clothes upon his back,
But he is rich in patience, and his temper is mild.
He walks on callous feet intimate with earth and sod,
But he is always in the presence of his ever-loving God.

Not For Me — Injustice

Though I'm mocked, looked down on,
Ridiculed, bear the scorn;
An outcast in my own world,
Marked for this since I was born;
Though pushed down into the mire,
Scorched and blistered by hate's fire,
I'll come out of it somehow,
But to injustice I'll not bow.

I'll bear the brunt of sword-like tongues,
Intent my being to harm;
If my character is tarnished
I will make no alarm.
My psyche, like a tower
Will withstand the rampant power
Of the strong, who will become weak
When I with courage speak.

Right, like a river, flows unchecked
And overcomes the wrong.
With hope in hand I'll persevere,
And courage makes me strong.
I will not remain downtrodden,
Though my cheeks from tears are sodden.
Injustice will not cloud my eyes,
Like mist off the lake, I'll rise.

Willful Lies

Like feathers in the wind they go,
Swift effortless and free.
Nor care about the truths they know,
Or what is their destiny.
They soar, alight, alight and soar,
Each ear they touch will be one more.

They fly unhindered if unchecked,
Straight from the liar's lips;
And hasten, hearts and lives to wreck,
Each feather wafts and dips,
Then settles for awhile, at least
Until the hearers end the feast …

Or fan the flames that will consume
One's character with greed,
Allowing freedom, ample room
To spread despair, with speed.
Lies gain success only when we
Give them the chances to be free.

Their dying depends on the wind
Of our encouragement.
We can deplore, ignore, rescind,
Till they're totally spent
Like feathers in the wind. They'll lie
Uncultivated, till they die.

Don't Blame Me

Don't blame me for errors I may make when I am depressed,
Or lamentations uttered from my mouth when sore distressed;
I'm only mortal, frail and weak
And expendable too;
I can't in Babelic tongues speak,
Or mysterious things do.
If nothing but disgust you see,
Then don't blame me.

Don't blame me if I raise my voice in anger on some days,
Or if you've found that I have changed towards you in some ways;
It might be that I do not even notice any change,
It might be that I am not aware of even acting strange.
My very own I may not know,
Or where I am not heed;
Acknowledgement I may not show,
Or even know I'm in need.
Sure, you may only pity see,
But don't blame me.

Don't blame me ever, it's no use to go against the grain,
To fight the odds I've no power over, or constantly complain;
I cannot help myself, I'm lost,
Most times don't know my name;
In every way I pay the cost,
But I am not to blame.
Alzheimer's the culprit, you see,
So don't blame me!

Leave Them Laughing

Leave them laughing. Don't discount
Their pleasures; let them mount and mount.
Even if it is at your expense.
If you let down your defence,
Laughter will, in time, for some,
Inhibitions overcome.
It works for woman or man,
Leave them laughing if you can.

Leave them laughing. If with hate
They set out to terminate
All the good that has been done,
And if remorse there is none,
Stand up with a will of steel,
Brace yourself until you feel
Pleasant wrinkles forming on
Your life's face, for anger is gone.

When you leave them laughing, they
Will have no choice but to obey.
For laughter is the food of the soul,
That can soothe the bent and whole.
Transform anger into peace,
A response that can increase.
Laughter can deter their wrath,
And straighten the tortuous path.

If blood is what your foes seek,
You can turn the other cheek
Blushed with laughter. Though you're not
Backing down, sound tools you've got.
You are showing them the way,
Without even a word to say.
As each in his conscience delves,
Leave them laughing at themselves.

On the Way to the O.R.

My first night in St. Joseph's as number 'Seven O Dash One,'
An adventure or an ordeal for me had just begun.
The other patient first me, she got the window bed,
So of course I had to settle for the outside one instead.

My supper, a small morsel, others would just call grub,
Then those confounded showers with that awful pre-op scrub.
Oh, yes, my back they painted with cold Proviodine,
But I would have felt much better if instead they'd given me wine.

A sleeping pill they gave me, which I swallowed with delight,
For I had no intentions of staying awake all night.
Next day I'm awakened early, it's the day of reckoning.
A fancy O.R. gown don and a weird-looking underthing.

An intravenous fluid is up to lubricate my vein,
And pre-op medication given to calm me down again.
Oh, yes, I've said my prayers, and spoken on the phone with Lou,
I'm thinking while I am waiting for there is nothing else to do.
I will keep my faith and trust that God is with me, for
They have come for me, I am now on my way to the O.R.

Listen to Learn

Not as roaring fires glow and glisten
While their embers heave and burn;
Sometimes we should just sit back and listen
And see how much we can learn.

Though the urge to speak out is intense,
Though you have a lot to say,
Listening to others does make sense,
And in time will make your day.

You will have to listen for to learn,
Shut out every din around.
For when you do, knowledge you will earn,
Though you have not made a sound.

Listen well to learn what is going on,
Hold your voice, open your ears.
You might even end up being the smart one;
A good listener always hears.

Election Rejection

Another election is called,
More tax money to waste;
No heed is paid to tide or flood,
The election is called in haste.

Diehards get on the bandwagon,
Their parties to promote;
And on our lawns placards appear,
Telling for whom to vote.

There's P.C. party, Liberal,
New Democrat, Reform;
And in Quebec they have the Bloc,
Which to them is the norm.

One party reeks of racism,
One wants to separate;
Work-fare and fingerprinting
Of the poor, one will create.

The middle class is overtaxed,
Thousands are out of work,
While politicians and their friends
Prosper and wear a smirk.

They all debate and advertise
About how well they'll do;
How they'll protect, restore, create
Edens for me and you.

But I've become cynical now,
No more on them will dote;
In fact, come next election day
I doubt that I will vote.

Love's Many Faces

It is made to appear cold and harsh
On the abuser's fists,
Before and after they land upon the victim's frailty;
Or with incestuous force,
A young child's screams are squashed,
As body, mind, and self esteem
Are bruised with the words 'I love you.'

'With my love I thee wed,' the couple pledges,
And seals this sensual love with a deep kiss,
As they merge willingly and become one,
And strive to fan the ember to a flame,
Which, with persistence, will keep love ablaze
To create an example fit to be displayed
For to see, all in the good name of love.

And as the baby looks deep into eyes
Of love, reflecting love and purest joy,
He smiles for the first time and thus evokes
Responsive love from mother, as she hugs
Her love, who nestles closely, from her drinks
The life source, whereby he's allowed to grow
Into a love child, bonded by her love.

Then solid friendship of the rarest kind
Can cause one to consent with not a thought of risk,
To go the length to help a friend in need,
Without counting the cost.
If love is kind, honest, tender, and should be nurtured to full bloom,
Then we must change it from just a mere word,
To a fruitful and model way of life.

Colour This Feeling Love

I feel all bubbly, bursting from within,
My mind is reeling, I am in a spin;
A healthy heart is brimful of pure joy,
And naught can ever this feeling annoy.
My spirit feels as free as clouds above;
Colour this feeling love.

I cannot contain the happiness I feel,
And pinch myself to prove that it is real.
Emotions mingle and shift like quicksand,
And over me they tend to take command.
Within, without, I feel free as a dove;
Colour this feeling love.

Colour my eyes, which mirror my self-worth,
Colour my countenance, which reflects mirth.
Colour the nimble way I move about,
Colour my voice, when with joy I do shout.
Colour the silent singing in my mind,
And here's what you'll find …

A spirit basking, full of hope and peace,
Serenity that is on the increase;
A mind that's calm and feeds it to the soul,
One unit that feels so complete and whole.
Fathomless as the sea, the sky above,
Colour this feeling love.

The Graduate — 1

He walks onto the podium,
Gowned, capped and with a smile.
The moment he had waited for
It seems, took a long while.
He now has the Honours B.A.
He's worked four years to earn,
But the working climate out there
Conjures up much concern.

A career he is eager to start,
But he does realize
That of the unemployed he's part,
And sadness fills his eyes.
The years of mental drudgery,
Anticipation, too,
Eagerness to join the work force —
Will all now go askew?

He has listened to the news. He's read
The papers, knows the score,
That the unemployment crisis,
Is now right at his door.
Every facet of all careers
Has been touched; workers are fired,
And with downsizing in business,
There's poor chance of him being hired.

But the sun is shining brightly
On his face but not his heart.
This is his moment, precious, rare,
When he will make his start.
The dignitaries' hands he shakes,
To the audience gives a bow.
As the cameras flash and cheers ring out,
The graduate thinks "What now?"

A Tribute to the Graduate

This is another milestone in your life we're glad to share,
And for that, we congratulate you now.
You strove for your Excelsior, even through times of stress and care;
You've surely earned the right to take a bow.

The new stage in your life that you have reached through diligence,
This prize that you have earned with fortitude,
Is yours to carry forward with insight and common-sense,
Into the work world, as you hoped you would.

Congratulations go out for the great work you have done,
For holding steadfastly on to the end.
Godspeed, good luck, we offer to the graduate, our son,
May life's good fortunes meet you round the bend.

And may you always move forward and upward every day,
Choosing the things in life that matter most.
And aim for just the best and what's important, all the way,
For all virtues become a willing host.

Literary Interrogation

She finds me among shelves
Of books set out in ordered lines.
Authors unknown to her, whose works
She sought within confines
Of a school project,
Important for earning a good grade.
Her searching brings her face to face with me,
She seeks my aid.
So I sit down and listen as she speaks,
And contemplate the answers that she seeks.

A Chance for Mankind

If we can live together as a people,
And not care what our colour is, or clan;
And not care what our class is, or what age group,
Whether each is a woman or a man …

If we can see each other as a person
Created by one God and so the same;
Each given one soul, one life and a purpose,
To love each other in the Saviour's name …

If we can find within our hearts, and always
The ability to help each other grow;
To lend a helping hand when it is needed,
And mercy and compassion always show …

If we can wear a smile when we are losing,
And our opponent can congratulate;
If we can offer praise when praise we merit,
And never one another e'er berate …

If we could borrow patience from the morning,
And harvest meekness from a baby's smile,
Then temper down our strengths with love and kindness,
And know that all our efforts are worthwhile …

If readily we all could be forgiving
Of those who have wronged us along the way,
And stem our anger, put joy back in living,
And soften every harsh word we may say …

If all our efforts are combined for goodness,
And all our words translate into pure truths,
If all of us would really make the effort,
And good examples set for all our youths …

If we all show respect and admiration
For all God's creatures, whether great or small,
If we can love and live love to the fullest,
There'd be a chance for mankind after all.

The Sea

The sea lies there beneath the sky, a part of earth,
A fluid mass, that cannot be controlled.
Wide at its widest and as deep, its shores, its berth,
And in its depths, secrets it won't unfold.
Goes where it wills, obeys no rules,
Nor satisfies the whims of fools.

A disembodied giant which can gentle be,
But in its time, refuses to be coaxed.
It owns its strength, is mighty in its might and free,
Cannot be tempered down, cajoled or hoaxed.
Its moods unfurl at its command,
And change, just like its drifting sand.

The Injured Gull

Like a loaf of bread, mired in the water, soggy,
He floats effortlessly, body is limp, looks groggy.
Not a sound he makes; perhaps he's too weak to cry.
Or maybe, in pain, he's much too shocked to try.
His focused gaze, eyes bright, strength not yet spent,
Because survival is his main intent.
His wing is broken, from a bullet or a stone.
He is now water-bound, and there may die alone.

Ode to a Blue-jay

You beauty with the raucous voice,
You woo me with your song.
And hearing you, I have no choice
But to listen all day long,
As you demand an audience
Whether they're near or far.
Viewing your beauty, they come hence
To see and hear the 'star.'

You watch me from your leafy perch
And I know that you're there.
You hop from limb to limb and search
With bright eyes, everywhere,
To see if I, perhaps, did leave
Some peanuts out for you;
Then down you swoop, the nuts retrieve,
And soar off beneath the blue.

I wonder, as you hop around
Or fly to summer skies,
How many, like me, you have found
To listen to your cries;
To feed you and admire you,
To hear each song you sing.
And perhaps they do miss you too
When you are on the wing.

I count the days till spring is here,
And you return once more,
To haunt my thoughts with sounds so dear,
Your songs to hear once more.
You pretty bird, bedecked in white
And blue, why don't you stay,
And with your beauty grace my sight,
When I awake each day?

The Arrival of Spring

Subtly spring has taken over the reins,
Forcing winter with its iron chains
Out the back door, banished from the scene,
Leaving behind grass that has turned green.

Bathed and puddled by the warm spring rain,
Earth is softening, ploughable again.
Trees are straightening up to see the sun,
And insects on branches, gauntlets run.

Birds arrive in flocks to build their nests,
Martins, jays, robins with scarlet breasts.
Butterflies flit by as if in search
Of a warm sunbeam on which to perch.

Early blossoming of orchard trees
Welcome with free nectar, migrant bees.
Hummingbirds hovering to get their share,
In some gardens are appearances rare.

Skies take on a deeper shade of blue,
Spring flowers show with grace their varied hue.
Breezes blow, touching with warmth, a sigh,
As they gently chase soft clouds on high.

Cotton-candy heaven, birds in song,
Shimmering willow branches whispering long.
Rain-moist rays touch swallows on the wing,
Heralding the arrival of spring.

For Springtime's Sake

When Spring is here,
And sky is clear,
And feeble steps are snappy,
When songbirds sing,
And everything
Is green, and hearts are happy,
That's when we tend to dream wild dreams,
And lose ourselves in idle schemes.

Just as the trees
Sway in the breeze,
And grass unfurls unhindered,
Our thoughts obey,
And join the fray,
As freely joy is tendered.
Then all life joyfully awake
And embrace spring, for springtime's sake.

For springtime's sake
Chances we take,
As life around us wakens,
As birds on wing
Their carols sing
And sleepy earth is shaken,
We blossom forth with zeal and zest,
For spring is the season most love best.

The Songbirds' Singing

On the threshold of each morning
Songbirds begin a new song;
Human hearts and ears adorning
All day long.

Hear them sing, their trills melodious
Through the spring and summer days,
Would such sounds stay warm and glorious,
Here, always!

Love the songbirds' cheerful singing,
Tells my heart that I can cope
With what fate to me is bringing,
And there's hope.

Songbirds stay within my hearing,
Fill my days with joy untold,
For it's winter that I'm fearing,
Its mute cold.

When you all go south and leave me
Here to pine, till you return,
It's your absence that does grieve me,
For spring yearn …

For once more I'll see your beauty,
Glory in your joyful strain;
Willingly you'll do your duty
Once again.

Summer Songs

Summer songs on summer days are heard everywhere,
And the echo always stays lingering on the air.
In the valley, on the hill,
Summer days are never still.
Summer sounds are haunting, long,
Heightened by each summer song.

Breezes stay in tune, as they touch the leafy strings
Of the trees, and they obey. Joyfully each sings.
And the gurgling of the brook
Tumbling past a forest nook.
Crackling sounds of snapping twigs,
And the chipmunks as they jig.

Choirs of birds rend the still air each morning at dawn,
Singing without fear or care, on a tree or lawn.
The music long and sweet,
To listeners ears a treat
That stays in the hearers' heart,
Never, never to depart.

Honey bees that hum and hum as they raid the flowers,
And the flies buzz as they come in our picnic bowers.
A bullfrog's croaky call,
A crashing waterfall;
Are the sweet notes that do belong,
With every lovely summer's song.

Summer Sounds

Summer sounds heard far and near
In woodland, dale and hill;
Loud whispers in the moonlight clear,
On dew-drenched mornings still.
Whistling through the woodland glen,
Soft breezes flick the blades
Of grass, and take the sounds of men
And hide them in the shades,
So they won't tarnish silvery trills
Of many lovely birds,
Or sounds of bees on flowering hills,
Or lowing of the herds
Grazing beside the gurgling streams —
Summer sounds like these fill my dreams.

Tropic Morning

The dew-drenched night gives birth to radiant morning,
As soft, still, white mist veils the deep green hills.
And filtering sunlight golden rays adorning,
As each warm sunray every crevice fills.

The sleepy valleys fringed on every border,
Show hazy rivulets winding their way
Past bamboo ridges, thickets, trimmed, in order,
As tropic leaves lift up to greet the day.

The perfumed air, seasoned with jasmine and spice,
Is stirred by gentle movements of the trees.
The lightless moon, shown only in its half-slice,
Hides beneath soft white clouds chased by the breeze.

And far and near, dogs bark and there's the crowing
Of roosting cocks, awakened hours before.
And always, nearby, the sea sound is growing,
As lazy salt waves lap against the shore.

And smoke from kitchens all around is rising,
As roasted breadfruits give up their good smell.
Brewed coffee, sage, or mint is emphasizing
A tropic country morning, known quite well.

The Sugarcane Cutter

Tiered bundles grace his head,
As homeward bound
His naked feet
The pavement pound,
So he can earn his bread.

And with each swishing sound,
The severed joints
Form bundles neat.
Then each road points
To market; joys abound!

The Garden Inside

It's not exactly a hothouse for plants
Not half as wide or even half as long,
Not the ideal spot a gardener wants,
But it satisfies an urge that is strong.
I take the summer and transplant it inside,
Give it water and some sunlight and care,
And when it does bloom, summer's beauty won't hide
In the dullness of old winter's stare.

Give Thanks All Year

There is so much in our daily lives that we should give thanks for,
And forget all distasteful things and those that we abhor,
The fact that we're alive,
The strength that makes us strive
To reach for our Excelsiors and know that they are sure.

The knowledge that there is a God who oversees each life,
Tempers our warring spirits as they tackle stress and strife.
Give us the courage to
Show strength in what we do.
We're duty-bound to praise Him on the harp or lute or fife.

Food of life that sustains us as we live from day to day,
And thanks for all our loved ones, and for friends made on the way.
For homes which shelter us,
And good things gathered thus
In our earth's harvest, through the years, in what we do and say.

We are a people blest with many bounties in our store,
And even those of us with much less than we had before
Should offer thanks as well,
For therein blessings dwell,
And thankfulness is one thing in which we should not be poor.

And so, not only on Thanksgiving Day should thanks be given,
And no one should be coaxed, cajoled, be forced or even driven
To offer thanks and praise,
Grateful voices raise,
Throughout the year, always, for all the blessings sent from heaven.

Autumn is Moving In

When frost is on the pumpkin and the wind blows strong and cold,
When rosy-fingered dawns embrace the days as they unfold;
When the leaves on all the trees on hills and vales begin to fall,
And the birds which occupied the skies and gardens cease to call,
When wind bruises exposed skin,
That's when autumn is moving in.

When mornings and evenings are dark and all the days
          are shorter too,
And there is a race for time in all the outdoor chores you do.
When you behold the dusting of white frost on browning grass,
And overhead, migrating birds in V-shaped columns pass,
Somehow, somewhere, deep within,
You know autumn is moving in.

When thin ice crystals crust the waters on the lakes and ponds,
And cold winds roughly caress trees, twisting their naked fronds;
And earth begins to harden and become like molten stone,
And on evergreens in woodland you cannot find one dry cone,
You'll know autumn has got the win,
It has simply moved right in.

White Silence

White silence that is so profound,
It resonates in perfect sound,
And mesmerizes all around
Who catches sight,
Of winter's beauty, held spellbound
By winter's white.

A landscape painted with fresh snow,
Attended only by winds that blow,
Or winter sun's warm daylight glow,
Nature's design.
After the snowstorm, what a show!
Almost divine!

At silent white I gaze in awe,
And marvel at old Nature's law,
Hoping the magic won't withdraw,
White silence free.
For nothing should such beauty flaw,
But pristine be.

Winter Lives

Winter lives in all its glory,
It holds on with all its might;
Grudgingly withholds the story
That behind it, things look bright.
In its greed it takes a foothold,
And grasps land and all therein,
With fingers agile and ice-cold,
Camouflaged by its white grin.

Fools the unsuspecting victims,
If one day it dormant lies.
Allows naïve souls their last whims;
It's disguised 'neath clear March skies.
Then when all is least suspecting,
Lashes out with real brute force;
Cutting winds, and snow collecting
On the ground's iced face, of course.

It's a stubborn, selfish season,
Full of rage, despite its smile;
And it's wondered, with good reason,
Why is it in nature's data file?
Ruthlessly it would erase spring,
Destroy all the joy Spring gives;
Its last song for now, it will sing;
Till that last note, winter lives!

Silent Sounds

No one ever need be vocal
To express what's in his heart,
Words are just simple protocol,
Voiced when ideas make a start.
All one's inner thoughts, each feeling,
Deep emotions, anger, joy,
Through his eyes, the mute appealing,
Subtle messages employ.

Language that is strong, convincing,
Bares the soul with just a glance,
Tells of pain in facial wincing,
Or love in a new romance.
One can tell his heart's desire,
And his secret thoughts make bare,
Through eyes, smiling or on fire,
Or a sullen, silent stare.

Silent sounds can, in a moment
Calm or rend a life or heart;
Love and gladness joyfully vent,
Or hatred and sorrow start.
May the words we say in silence
Through our eyes, be always found
To provoke a deep love, and hence
Echo through each silent sound.

Winter Blues

I woke up late and my temperament was rather sour,
I had to be at work for six and it was past the hour.
The red digits on my clock radio were flashing "nine,"
I tried to calm my rigid nerves by stating I'd be fine.
I donned my coat, my hat and gloves, and wished I had heard
                                                    the news,
Then walked outside and discovered that I needed snowshoes.

That meant I had to shovel snow, my arms and back did ache;
I toiled for fifty minutes, then discovered my mistake.
I had cleaned the car off nicely, but I did not think to start
It before I began shovelling; that surely was not smart.

Of course the car refused to budge, the battery was dead,
My hands and feet were frozen, and the pounding in my head
Was more than I could bear; I had to throw the towel in.
I was fighting a battle that I knew I wouldn't win.
I limped inside the house shivering. I needed no more clues,
I was the helpless victim, on that day, of winter blues.

Squirrels at Play

It was on a sunny winter's day,
With snow deep on the ground,
That I espied, in frisky play,
Two forms furry and round.
Two squirrels caused my eyes to stay
Upon their antic forms,
Compelling me to look their way,
And shun my daily norm.

In the soft snow their tails imprint
As to and fro they'd run
And somersaulted in the glint
Of light from winter's sun.
Two furry shapes, both wild and free,
The squirrels firmly clung
To naked branches of the tree,
For minutes, limply hung.

Then dropping lightly to the ground,
Then leaping on the fence,
And making not a single sound
As they scurried thence.
They romped and played minutes on end,
So free and without care;
Did they perhaps, a message send
To me, as I stood there?

My daily chores neglected, but
My mind felt more at ease,
Relaxed; my day's routine was cut
From boredom, if you please!
My regimented hours were fixed,
Until that winter's day
I watched unhindered (feelings mixed)
Two squirrels at their play.

Shrouding of the Trees

In cold ice cloaks encrusted,
Each branch, each naked twig,
So intimate, entrusted,
The trees wear their ice wigs.
Embraced in winter's ice shrouds,
Nor scorn its cold embrace,
Beneath the menacing clouds
Their consummation face.

Nor fearing nor retreating
From nature's wanton kiss,
The trees accept the fleeting
Ecstatic taste of bliss,
Offered in such abundance
In a few short wintry hours,
By a lover, whose preponderance
Of force, enriches his power.

The icy consummation
Is brief, as it nears spring.
A silent affirmation
To love's cold endearing.
And so late winter's shrouding
Of the trees in crystal white,
Prepare them for the crowding
Of their leaves when weather's bright.

Winter's Last Breath

Winter's last breath of fury,
Hurls havoc on the land,
It shows the world its power
As it takes full command.

It glazes trees and fences
With ice so crystal clear,
Offers the ground a blanket
It can't refuse to wear.

For walking, it is treacherous,
Uncomfortable, cold;
But oh, the latent icing
Is beauteous to behold.

When the snow melts, it washes
The land, the trees, the air;
As it helps them get ready
For spring and summer fair.

Though its last breath is furious,
And may cause some concern,
Some of us, in mid-summer,
Will for old winter yearn.

Return of the Red-winged Blackbirds

They chatter with excitement
To each other, to the air,
As they crowd the treetops, fidgeting,
Telling me they are there.

Swoop down in unison upon
The feeder and the ground;
Gobble in haste the grain they find
That's scattered all around.

Having eaten, but far from filled,
They rest awhile, and chatter long,
They make me wait for warmer days
Before sharing their song.

But I am glad to see them
Nonetheless, they are the sights
Which tell me that old winter
Has finally taken flight.

That spring is on the threshold,
That she opens up with grace
Nature's soft curtains, warm and bright,
Flooding light in every place.

Red-winged blackbirds are surely
Harbingers of spring to me,
And that is why, on winter's cusp
I am thrilled when one I see.

Soaring Spirit

It soars like the seagull,
On warm uplifting air.
It rises high,
Up in the sky,
Like feathered wings,
Or metal things.
The whispering winds seem to lull
It, as it soars without a care.

It's like the kite of childhood
Made of paper and of strings.
It soars there,
On the air,
Not red and blue,
Or gummed with glue,
But light as cork and strong as wood,
Free spirit soars and lifts and swings.

The Wrong Queue

I watch the buses as they sit
Idling in a neat row.
I watch them watch me watching them,
And wonder how I'll know
Which one will be the GO Express,
Which will take me to where
I'm bound, for I must leave real soon,
I must leave soon from here.

And so I wait impatiently
On platform number eight.
Silently, I pray one will move soon,
And cross to where I wait.
The queue is longer now, the wind
Blows cold against my knees,
And if the bus does not come now,
I just might start to freeze.

At last a driver enters one,
And slowly takes his seat.
He starts the engine, let it run,
Then goes and checks each seat.
He sits behind the wheel now, great!
At last he's pulling out,
The bus now stops in front of me,
"You took your time!" I shout.

"I must be in Toronto for
A very special date,
And it is now ten past the hour,
Which means that you are late!"
"This bus goes to Niagara Falls,
You're on the wrong platform!
And I am right on schedule, Ma'am,
You're the one south of norm."

I slink out of the line and try
Embarrassment to hide.
The cold wind hits my flustered cheeks,
And mocks my dented pride.
I move along and scan the buses
As I pass them, to see
The one that is Toronto bound.
There it is, in front of me!

I am fifteenth in the queue now,
And the boarding has begun.
I tell myself I'll make the date
Before this day is done!

A Difficult Decision

I pick you up reluctantly and pause,
I do not want to carry out the task
That has fallen to me.
A job that I did not beg for, nor ask,
But what will surely be.

You've been a trusted friend, a source of rest,
An oasis of ease for aching back,
For tired legs, the best.
When daily chores, muscles and mind attack,
I was your willing guest.

We came together on my wedding day,
And we grew close as years flew quickly by.
Our aging had begun.
But you continued, or at least did try,
Ere your last song was sung.

Now we are old, we are being forced apart,
And now I have to do what I must do,
This grave indignity,
A parting of the ways for me and you,
Has come, reluctantly.

You will be forced to go, and by my hands,
And I wonder if you were in my place,
Would you quickly unload
Me like unwanted garbage, in disgrace
Out there, beside the road?

Candid Thoughts

Black Canadians —
Part of the Canadian Family Tree

February is Black history and heritage month in Canada and the United States. It is a good time for the black population of this country to pause and reflect upon the part it has played over the years, and the varied and very valuable contributions it has made to our Canadian heritage.

From 1606 (the date of arrival of Matthieu da Costa, thought to be the first black person to set foot on Canadian soil), to the present, black people have left and are leaving their mark on the Canadian soul.

The presence of blacks as domestic slaves in Canada began as early as the 1600s in Quebec, which was called Port Royal. These were followed by a number of escaped slaves from the U.S., coming into Upper and Lower Canada via the Underground Railway, helped by such conductors as Harriet Tubman and Josiah Henson. Over 3,000 blacks from the U.S. who had fought for the British in the Revolutionary War of 1755–1783 arrived as loyalists in Nova Scotia. Among them was an entire army corps known as the Black Pioneers. When the British reneged on their promise of land and freedom for the black loyalists, some of them became disillusioned and, under the leadership of Thomas Peters, left the seaboard provinces for resettlement in Sierra Leone, West Africa in 1792.

In 1800, they were followed by a group of about 600 Jamaican Maroons who had been deported from Jamaica by the British because they refused to be enslaved. Those remaining put down roots and tried to manage as best they could.

Blacks from the American west coast also settled in Vancouver and by 1860 the Canadian black population was about 60,000. During the land rush period of 1890–1914, American blacks, coming mainly from Oklahoma, resettled in Saskatchewan and areas like Amber Valley in Alberta, which has remained a predominantly black community.

These early settlers, especially those living in Ontario (in communities such as Buxton, Chatham, Dresner, Windsor and Hamilton) excelled in business and trade. They built their own houses, schools, and churches, many of which remain in good condition after nearly 200 years. Examples include Josiah Henson's house in Buxton, the First Baptist Church in Windsor, and Stewart Memorial Church in Hamilton. Some grew cash crops; in Dawn, near Chatham, was a 1500-acre farm growing tobacco, wheat, and oats, organized by Josiah Henson, among others. In this community, they even had their own sawmill and brickyard. On the Prairies, some, such as John Ware, became successful ranchers, and in British Columbia, a few men, such as Henry McDame, were successful gold prospectors.

Many heads of families were small businessmen and skilled workers. Soon, bakeries, barber and tailor shops, and restaurants were set up. Two newspapers, were owned and operated by blacks: the *Voice of the Fugitive*, and *Provincial Freeman*, a controversial paper edited by Mary Ann Shadd. Ms. Shadd, through her newspaper columns, spoke out against segregation and emphasized the need for new black Canadians to have self-worth, self-reliance, and pride in their new country. Henson, through his preaching and teachings and his autobiography, *The Life of Josiah Henson*, also helped to motivate and encourage the new settlers who were facing blatant discrimination and injustice from whites.

In 1910, the *Immigration Act*, which allowed for selection of immigrants along racial lines, brought about a reduction in the flow of black immigration.

Canadians of West Indian origin come largely from the former British West Indies, which include Jamaica, Barbados, Trinidad and Tobago, St. Kitts and Nevis, Grenada, St. Lucia, Antigua, and Guyana, all being members of the British Commonwealth. These people are of diverse racial backgrounds and share the same cultural characteristics, as well as similar climate, history, and political background. West Indians are accustomed to striving for better standards of living, and over 130,000 have immigrated to Canada since 1946. Of this number, 86 percent settled in Ontario, with the majority in Toronto, Hamilton and their region. Many came as university students and on graduation applied for landed immigrant status. Whereas in the early 1960s most immigrants from the Caribbean (including Haitians) were confined to the services, recreation, clerical and skilled group categories, a very high percentage of West Indian immigrants in 1972–1974 were managerial and professional people.

Haitian immigrants have settled mostly in Quebec because, as francophones, they find it easier to settle in there. A medical centre opened in Quebec in the late 1970s is staffed primarily by Haitian doctors, and a Québécois of Haitian origin was elected to the National Assembly as a member of the Parti Québécois in November, 1976.

African immigration (from Nigeria, Angola, South Africa, Kenya, Uganda, and Ghana) is fairly recent, although small numbers studied here as early as the 1930s. About four-fifths of immigrants from Africa today are registered students in colleges and universities. The majority have settled in Toronto and surrounding areas, but some also live in Halifax, Quebec, Calgary, Edmonton, and Victoria. Some Africans, such as Somalis, have recently arrived as refugees because of political unrest in their country.

There are a number of established organizations in and around black communities that provide cultural and recreational activities for their members, as well as speaking out on issues affecting all of the black communities. A few such organizations are the Afro-Canadian Caribbean Association of Hamilton and District, The Negro Citizenship Association of Montreal, the Trinidad and Tobago and Jamaica Canadian Associations of Toronto and The Black Historical and Cultural Society of British Columbia, all under the umbrella of the National Black Coalition of Canada. These organizations also work to ease settlement for new arrivals, to promote culture, and to acquaint Canadians with their cultures.

It has been a long, rough road from the first black settlers' arrival in this country to the present, and we have made some strides down it. A large number of blacks have added their presence in the professions (nursing, teaching, law, medicine), in politics, in art and entertainment, in journalism, sports, business, and literature. We have learned a lot during our process of growth, but still need to realize that our identity as black Canadians will continually be in danger of becoming lost if we do not consolidate our efforts, loyalty, pride, and love. The focus is unity.

We are black Canadians regardless of when we arrived, or from where. We have all contributed to the growth and prosperity of this nation. And despite the prejudices, injustices, and discrimination that still exist in our society today, we will continue to contribute ungrudgingly to the Canadian heritage, knowing for a fact that we are indeed a very sturdy branch on the Canadian family tree.

Some Black-Canadian Firsts

Professions

Gwenyth Barton and **Ruth Bailey:** First black women to graduate from a Canadian school of nursing, 1948.

Wilson Brooks: Toronto's first black public school teacher.

Violet King: First black woman to practise law in Canada, 1954.

Ed Searles: First black lawyer to be admitted to the bar in British Columbia in 1957.

Selwyn Romily: B.C.'s first black judge, 1974.

Lionel Jones: First black man to be admitted to the bar in Alberta, 1963.

David Pollanis: First black police officer in Regina, 1969.

Stanley Grizzle: Canada's first Federal Citizenship Court Judge, 1976.

Delos Rogest Davis: First black appointed King's Counsel in Amherstburg, Ontario, 1910.

Religion

Rev. Addie Aylestock: First black woman to be ordained, 1951.

Wilbur Howard: First black United Church of Canada Moderator, 1974.

Politics

Mifflin Gibb: First black to be elected to Victoria City Council in 1800.

Lincoln Alexander: First black to be elected to the Parliament of Canada 1968; first black to become Lieutenant Governor of Ontario.

Emery Barnes and **Rosemary Brown:** First black members of the B.C. legislature, 1972.

Leonard Braithwaite: First black man elected to the Ontario Legislature, 1964.

Dr. Monestime: First black mayor of Mattawa, Ontario, 1958.

Dr. Daniel Hill: Director of the first Human Rights Commission in Canada, 1961.

Media

Voice of the Fugitive: The first black newspaper in Canada, founded by **Henry Bibb** in 1851 and published until 1854.

The Provincial Freeman: Founded by **Samuel Ward** in 1853, edited by **Mary Ann Shadd**. Last issue was published in 1857.

Mary Ann Shadd: First black woman journalist in North America.

Elnora Collins: First Canadian female artist to have a TV series named after her — "The Elnora Show" in British Columbia.

Michael Williams: Canada's first laserist. (He added special effects to TV productions and rock concerts.)

Military

William Hall: First black to be awarded the Victoria Cross for bravery. He fought with the British Regiment in India in the 1800s.

Percy Haynes: First black petty officer in the Canadian Navy, during World War II.

The #2 Construction Battalion: The first all-black battalion in Canadian history, formed in 1916.

Sports

Willie O'Ree: First black player in the National Hockey League.

Harry Jerome: Track and field star, received the Order of Canada Medal in 1971.

Agriculture

John Ware: First to introduce Longhorn cattle in Canada, 1882, and one of the first to hold a rodeo.

Organizations

The Canadian League for the Advancement of Coloured People was formed 1924 by **Jenkins**, of London, Ontario, and **W. Montgomery** of Toronto.

National Black Coalition, formed in 1969 in Ontario.

The National Organization of Immigrant and Visible Minority Women of Canada, formed in Winnipeg in 1986.

To Our Black Youths — Yours is the Task

We all know black is beautiful, worthy, capable, proud;
Don't ever tarnish it by being lascivious and loud,
And don't let anyone convince you that you're not first-class.
Because you're black, there always will be barriers to bypass,
And you can overcome them all if steadfast you remain,
Believing in yourselves and for yourselves respect to gain.

Be kind and tolerant to all, especially to your own;
Be loving and considerate, let be honesty be shown.
Aim high in all you do. Only your very best will last,
For you're the precious link between our future and our past.
We did our best in years gone by to reach where we are now,
But you're our future; yours is the task to see it through somehow.

It will not be an easy road, the inclines might be steep;
There'll be times when sheer frustration will be enough to
make you weep.
Press on with pride, determination, and courage all the way.
Harvest your strengths to face each fight and live your lives each day.
With each other co-operate, come together at length;
Pool your efforts, love, resources, for unity is strength.

There is not much that we can give you, except love, encouragement,
That inherent fighting spirit, and, the chance your views to vent.
These are bases you can build on, these are sound, worthwhile gifts,
Use them to build your friendships and banish discords and rifts.
Strive for justice, peace, and freedom, honesty in all you do;
You owe it to your children, just as we owe it to you!

Moving Upwards Together

How important is the month of February to us all?
How significant is it to everyone?
Is it just a month to look back in our history and recall
The achievements of all those who have passed on
From the pioneer trails of yesteryears?
Do we ponder all their joys and fears?

Do we view it as a special time when all should pause and think
Of where we have come from, and where we will go?
Of what we can do as a people who are standing on the brink,
With our future in our hands, and much to know?
Shouldn't we use it as our foundation stone
To move up together, instead of alone?

For this time helps us to find ourselves, know each weakness and
strength,
Avoid past mistakes and hold each other's hand.
Be a family, a people working on the same wavelength
To achieve our goal, the prize, the promised land.
Fractious thoughts and actions at last tossed aside,
As we move upwards together, all in stride.

April is No Fool's Month

When one talks about the month of April, one automatically thinks of April Fool's Day, or All Fool's Day, as it is known in some parts of the world. It is the one day of the year when friends and relatives can play practical jokes, which are designed to be harmless and amusing, on each other.

But April is a much more important month than most people give it credit for. It was called Aprilis in the Roman calendar. At that time it was the second month of the year, having twenty-nine days, but Julius Caesar changed it in 46 B.C., and gave it an extra day. However, in the northern hemisphere, April is the first full month of spring and the fourth month of the year.

April is noted for copious amounts of rain — the famous April showers that we sing about. The rain is required to moisten the earth, swell the grains, and enable the seedlings to protrude through the soil into the sunlight.

In the northern hemisphere, April brings back greenery to the land. The grass sheds its yellow-brown winter dress, and dons velvet green. Trees that were dry and bare now show life in the tender buds and tiny leaves that appear on their branches.

Some flowering trees, such as the lilac, apple and cherry will blossom, welcoming the butterflies and bees to partake of their sweet nectar. Farmers and gardeners everywhere sow seeds in prepared fields and garden patches, and tulips and daffodils show off their gorgeous colours, adding beauty to the once-drab scenery.

In April, the migratory birds make their way back from tropical climes. The robins are usually the first to show up in gardens, hopping about on the lawns and singing at will. Then come the red-winged blackbirds, the grosbeaks, and the finches, joining the cardinals and mourning doves that winter here. They are all eager to reclaim their particular part of the trees that they used the year before, to start nest building, and to get on with the job of raising their young.

Religious holidays such as Good Friday, Easter and the Jewish Passover are usually observed in April. At this time of year, children (and sweet-toothed adults) can pig out on chocolate bunnies and Easter eggs, and women who adore hats can go on millinery buying sprees and blame it on the time of the year.

In Canada and the United States, Daylight Saving Time begins on the first Sunday in April. This is when we put our clocks forward, giving us an extra hour of daylight — something that the farmers welcome.

April is associated with certain notable scientific discoveries, such as the discovery of the North Pole on April 6, 1909 by Admiral Robert Perry. Also on April 12, 1961, Russian cosmonaut Yuri Gagarin was the first human to orbit the earth in a space capsule. The polio vaccine, discovered by American Dr. Jonas Salk, was declared to be effective in the treatment of poliomyelitis on April 12, 1955.

On April 20, 1940, the electron microscope was first publicly presented, and American Dr. Evarts Graham accomplished the first surgical removal of a lung in St. Louis, Missouri, on April 5, 1933.

Apart from my grandmother (who insisted that she came up with the idea of the vinegar-and-brown-sugar gargle as a cure for sore throats), many famous people were born in the month of April. The English poet William Shakespeare was born on April 23, 1564, and died on his birthday fifty-two years later.

Leonardo da Vinci, the Italian artist and scientist, was born on April 15, 1452, and the notorious dictator Adolf Hitler was born on April 20, 1889. The Monarch of Great Britain and the British Commonwealth, Queen Elizabeth II, was born on April 21, 1926. Another famous person with an April birthday was the black American educator Booker T. Washington, who was born on April 5, 1856.

April is also noted for certain disasters. The great San Francisco earthquake happened on April 18 and 19, 1906. Several hundred people were killed and there were millions of dollars in property damage and loss.

On April 15, 1912, the luxury liner Titanic struck an iceberg near Newfoundland and sank, killing more than 1500 people. Among other noteworthy events, the new African nation of Tanzania was formed by joining Tanganyika with Zanzibar on April 26, 1964, and Italian dictator Benito Mussolini was executed on April 28, 1945.

Flooding of rivers and streams is common in April because of torrential rains and freak snowstorms.

April means different things to different people. When asked what April meant to him, my son, then in his teens, replied without hesitation, "Two months to summer vacation." To a good friend of the family, April meant having done her income tax returns, with the hope of getting a refund.

Those of us who have birthdays in April, can at least boast about the gems representing the month, even if most cannot afford to own them — the diamond (a girl's best friend), and the sapphire. The daisy and the sweet-pea are the flowers of the month. We can also relate to the ram or the bull, depending on what part of the month we were born in. Both are formidable signs of the zodiac.

Although it is not the most popular month for weddings, many do take place in the month of April, and of course, as happens during other months of the year, babies will be born, and people will die in April, all over the world.

April then can be regarded, not only as the month in which April Fool's Day is celebrated, but as the beautiful, (though weatherwise it can be downright ugly), interesting and important month of the year that it really is.

Easter Happenings

It's Easter time and baby chicks
Are symbolic of the day.
Live bunny rabbits hop and skip
In warrens, where they stay;
And Easter lilies are in bloom,
What sweet perfusion in my room!

Assorted Easter baskets, filled
With goodies, grace the stores,
And children, so excited, thrilled,
More than the year before,
With busy hands and eager legs,
They search with zest for Easter eggs.

And sweet-toothed adults, children eat
Till their appetites are filled
With chocolate bunnies, what a treat
For weak, as the strong-willed.
Of course, there are Easter parades
Which from one's memory never fade.

And Easter murals grace some walls,
On some floors lie Easter mats;
Easter painting contests in some malls,
For some ladies, Easter hats.
And on Easter Sunday, church bells ring,
And the choirs with gladsome voices sing.

Contemplating Easter

We see the Easter lily,
And marvel at the sight;
How beautiful and pure it looks
How tender, soft, and white.
And we think of Easter
And the meaning of it all,
Then we know deep within each heart
That we must heed God's call.

For it is for the likes of us
That there's an Easter day,
That our dear Saviour walked for us
The entire Calvary way.
And that He did bleed and die,
The very reason He was born,
Life for us He reclaimed on high
That glorious Easter morn.

As children of our loving God,
As Christians who are blest,
We come in joyful fellowship
To attend this Easter fest.
May our Saviour's life and death,
His rising from the grave,
His holy unction ever fill
The souls He died to save.

And may we cherish in our hearts,
That Love that sets us free,
The Love that gave so willingly
That day on Calvary's tree.
And may our lives and living
Be a testament, confessed
Not just today, but always;
May love be our Easterfest.

"Mother" is Much More Than a Word

On the lips and in the thoughts of most of us in the "darling month of May" is the word Mother.

In some dictionaries, the word means "female parent," "natural," "inborn," and "originator of." The word is written differently in various languages (*madre* in Spanish; *mutter* in German; *mater* in Latin), but the meaning is the same. In English-speaking societies, the informal form of the word mother may be *mom, mummy, mommie,* or *mama*. But mother is much more than a word. It is a symbol of love, understanding and caring. It is a symbol of family and home.

The second Sunday of May is set aside in such countries as North America, Mexico, the English-speaking Caribbean islands, India, Sweden and Great Britain, for mothers to be honoured. This tradition was a proposal of Anna Jarvis of Grafton, West Virginia. As a result, the first Mother's Day celebration was held in Philadelphia on May 10, 1908. The idea quickly became popular throughout North America and other countries.

We use this day to show our mothers how much we care for them. Those of us whose mothers are living often wear a pink or red rose or carnation on that day, while those whose mothers are deceased wear white.

We take our mothers out to dinner or prepare their favourite meal and make it a family affair. We give them flowers, cards, gifts, and candies. We immortalize them in poetry and songs. We hug and kiss them and tell them that they are loved.

But our mothers have held and loved us throughout our dependent years and sometimes beyond that. For even in our adult lives we are considered their children. They have nursed and soothed, have gone without many times because of us. They have stayed up many nights to comfort us through illnesses and have allayed our fears through many vivid nightmares. They have been there for us when all else failed. And when we even doubted ourselves, they believed in us. All this love and caring took place continuously, not just on certain special days of the year.

Why then is it that so many mothers are left to pine away on their own in some lonely rooming house or nursing home? How is it so many never see or hear from their children for months and years unending? Why do they die alone? Should not we, their children to whom they gave all, reciprocate?

We should show our mothers that we love and care for them, not only on Mother's Day, but as often as possible while we have them with us in this life. If we are separated geographically, we should keep in touch by phone, by mail, by visits whenever possible. We should give them simple but worthwhile things like our hugs, flowers, and our listening ears.

Let us fill them with our kindness and love. Let us demonstrate that we are aware that *mother* is not only a word, it is a symbol of life. After all, if it were not for our mothers, would we have even been here?

A Tribute to Mothers

Mother is the gift God gave to mankind at the start,
A special person who of the alpha family was a part.
Nurtured us before she knew us, loves us until death,
With us her devotion lingers right to the last breath.
She unites the family unit, holds it fast and strong
With love and determination; we to her belong.

Mother comes in various colours, black, red, yellow, white;
And the love she gives her children borders on delight.
Never is she ever too busy to perform a task,
And her answers are forthcoming to questions we ask.
More often than not, her life she lays down on the line
In our defence; nor even death would she decline.

She is there in times of hardships, trouble, fear, and pain,
And the erring ones, her tender heart forgives again.
Suffers deeply when we suffer, in our joys diffused,
Often for our sakes, she is mistreated and abused.
But she never wavers in her love and in her care
For the ones she brought into the world her love to share.

Mother is everything to everyone. She is unique,
She's a source of strength, although within she may feel weak.
She's a friend, a nurse, a teacher, a playmate, a guide,
She's that person we trust and in whom we can confide.
She's a counsellor, our advocate, and when she prays
We are always in her prayers and will be through all our days.

Mother is a word depicting patience, caring, love,
Tolerance, unselfishness and peace, as of a dove;
Understanding, kindliness, and strength to overcome:
Mother means a family, and *Mother* means a home.
So to all mothers on Mother's Day, we'll raise a cheer,
Because without you, Mothers, none of us would be here.

I Am Woman!

The sons and daughters of the world I bear,
Though I was made from man.
I spin and weave the garments that they wear,
For their future have a plan!
I am woman.

I sorrow for my children lost in death,
I beat my breast and moan.
My love for them is strong to my last breath,
They are never alone,
Though I am gone.

My sunken eyes are testaments to love
When sorrow intervenes.
Many are the times my eyes are cast above,
And I know what loving means.
I'm in its scenes.

This woman lives and breathes her title, and
Will strive to keep it so.
My destiny I hold here in my hand,
Wherever I choose to go,
For I *am* woman.

Let's Give Fathers Their Due

For every biological human mother on the planet earth, there is a biological father. But fatherhood extends beyond the biological realms to include a social, psychological, and spiritual bonding between fathers and their children. A bond which, if allowed to blossom and grow by continued nurturing, will cause the father–child relationship to become steadfast.

The process of bonding is easier to accomplish in a mother–child relationship because of a child's dependency on the mother during the first few years of extrauterine life. This relationship is also possible with fathers and their children, but it is necessary as well as important that the fathers be there, and be physically involved in the children's upbringing, so that the interchange of love, trust, and understanding can develop mutually.

There are many fathers who, for various reasons, are regarded as being unfit. They may be abusive and neglectful towards their children, and some may play little or no role in their upbringing. But for every one of these types of fathers, there are hundreds who are not only breadwinners, but are loving, caring fathers, sensitive to the needs of their families, and willing to lay down their lives in order to provide for and protect them.

The traditional role of fathers as head of the households and breadwinners has been extended to something more tangible in today's society. Fathers now have, and accept the opportunity to begin bonding with their children while in utero. They attend pre-natal classes with their partners. They listen to the foetus's heart-beats and feel its movements. They can be, and often are, present at their child's birth and are eager and willing to share in such tasks as feeding, burping, changing, and bathing, and at times babysitting them. They eventually become relaxed and at ease with this role, and the bonding process between them and their children becomes spontaneous and total as it is with mothers. In fact, an involved father helps the entire family to bond.

Such fathers are the ones who rise at four o'clock in the morning to wait in line for hours in order to register their children in the local minor hockey, soccer, or baseball league. They are the ones who are at every (or almost every) game. The ones who volunteer (or are volunteered) to transport their children and other members of the teams to and from games and practices. The ones who are zealous with their cheering and encouragement. The ones who arduously help their youngsters practise that certain swing, or throw, or catch. Who are never too tired to take their daughters to singing or piano lessons, or to listen with patience to a babbled complaint and wipe a tearstained face. To help a child solve a tricky math problem, assemble or plan a science project, or to offer modest advice to a lovelorn teenager.

In most cases, these fathers carry out such activities quietly, through many years, with not so much as a "Thank you, Dad." However it is not because the children are ungrateful. They love their dads, are proud of them, and are never shy to boast about how clever and great they are. But in today's society, bad deeds seem to attract more attention than the good ones, and fathers who are loving, caring, and supportive of their families are often ignored and left standing on the fringes of recognition. It seems a natural thing for kids to take their dads for granted. They will readily hug and kiss Mom with little or no prompting, but not a thing for Dad! No "thank you," no handshake nor hug.

Although such neglect of fathers is not always intentional, it must be understood that fathers are people, too. They, like everyone else, would enjoy a compliment or two now and then. Why do we not make the effort to acknowledge them as often as we can?

Examples can be set for children in their early years of life, by having the mother complimenting the dad in the child's presence on how good he was with Junior. Also by encouraging children to express their appreciation by saying, "Thank you, Dad," and giving him a hug.

Fathers will not likely ask for recognition, but when they receive it, it makes a world of difference. It will put a bounce into their steps. It will make them feel worthwhile and needed, and reassure them that they are indeed an integral part of the family and will continue to be, long after the children have grown and moved away.

Let us give fathers their due.

Fathers Should Also Be Cherished

No one seems to realize or even want to very much
Know how important to each family fathers are.
The special parts they play, and each father's needed touch
Often makes him to his family a "star."
But though he might be adored,
Efforts are oft-times ignored,
Or maybe taken for granted
If the family's love is slanted
Towards the mother.
But he often takes it in stride,
Holds his disappointments inside
With no bother.

Fathers often are on the sidelines without wanting to be there,
They would rather be involved and not forgotten.
Though times have changed, fathers are not supposed to weaken
or show fear,
And if they do, they are dubbed as being rotten.
Fathers have so much to give
To their families while they live;
They just need some reassurance,
Need patience and long endurance,
To stay ahead.
And love from their loved ones, always,
And occasionally, some praise,
Laurels, instead.

Good role models fathers must be, always, in their children's eyes;
As a source of strength, they must be there for them.
Fatherhood is a blessed task, each dad should realize
That each son or daughter is a precious gem.
Love them and they'll love you too;
With them find neat things to do;
Be their father as well as friend,
To their every need attend,

And with them share.
Loving bonds they will not sever,
They will cherish you forever
And show they care.

The Tiny Victims of Drug Abuse

The increase in the use of illegal drugs among women of child-bearing age is today a worrying factor for members of the health-care system, especially those who work with newborn babies. Babies born to drug-addicted mothers are at grave risk.

It has become a common phenomenon on neonatal wards to see newborn babies displaying signs of drug withdrawal as early as half an hour after their birth. Through no fault of their own, these babies have been victims of drug abuse from the time of their conception to the hour of their birth.

Because of the potency of these drugs and the relatively small body surface of the foetus, drugs readily enter all foetal body cells at a very early stage of development. The effect is traumatic, and uterine growth and development is adversely affected.

Many foetuses abort spontaneously, and those that continue to term are usually growth-retarded and anaemic. Many have physical defects; some are infected with AIDS or other diseases. Many pregnancies end in stillbirth.

It is heart-rending to watch newborn babies in the throes of drug withdrawal. Infants with Neonatal Withdrawal Syndrome have rapid, laboured breathing, a continuous high-pitched cry, jerky limb movements, and sometimes convulsions. They are hyperactive, jittery and tense, especially when handled. They feed poorly, even though they may act hungry. They may have vomiting, diarrhoea, fever and sweating. These infants will later typically have growth and behavioural disturbances.

Many of these unfortunate babies are born to mothers who have the misfortune of finding themselves at the bottom of the social ladder. They more often than not are single, poorly educated, and very ignorant of the devastating effects their drug habits have on their babies' health and well-being. They are careless with their own health and eating habits, and some do not even present themselves to clinics or their doctors for much-needed prenatal care.

In some cases, maternity health-care givers are unaware of the mothers' drug use until the babies start displaying signs of withdrawal. The horrible thing about all this is that not all drug-induced harm will be evident at birth.

A baby will show signs of withdrawal from drugs such as heroin, morphine, barbiturates, alcohol, and tobacco; yet with cocaine, hashish and marijuana there won't be any signs, and the infant can suffer irreparable damage to the central nervous system before help can be given.

Health-care givers have the grim task of tackling the problem, trying to put right the wrong done to these innocent babies by their mothers.

Good, constant initial nursing care is critical to help ease the pain and discomfort these babies must feel during periods of withdrawal. They are handled as little as possible to avoid inducing convulsions. They are covered loosely with blankets and given pacifiers to cut down the crying. Their vital signs are constantly monitored, and they are fed through feeding tubes or intravenously. If supportive care is insufficient, then sedatives are given guardedly.

Because of the risk of Sudden Infant Death Syndrome (SIDS), and physical abuse of these babies, follow-up care is very important. Home monitoring systems are used, and social services must be involved to make sure that these babies do not fall prey to other abuses.

Much more is needed to be done, however, to try to lessen the occurrence of drug abuse and its complications in these babies. Members of the communities in which these tragedies occur so often need to get involved.

It is very important to be able to identify young women who are at risk, and give them the understanding, counselling, care, and teaching they need to help them realize the dangers of their drug abuse, and the severe consequences their babies have to pay for this abuse.

After all, these tiny victims of drug abuse depend not only on the health-care givers but on all of us to help protect and care for them. We must continue the battle to try to eradicate from our midst the disease known as drug abuse. We owe it to ourselves and to the tiny victims.

Flowers Say it All

Have you ever looked at a flower in the height of the growing season and ponder over its presence in your garden or field? How beautiful a show they make wherever they are seen! And what a waste it seems, and what disappointment we feel when they wither and die in the late months of the year!

Looking at flowers has become one of my favourite pastimes. I have always loved flowers and flowering trees, whether wild or cultivated. After all, they are a part of nature's wonderland — the essence of the great outdoors, at least in my opinion. And I happen to enjoy, without reservation, the great outdoors.

Recently however, I have begun to equate flowers with human mortality, and in a number of ways I am tempted to compare flowers and the human life cycle, with some fascination.

In our Christian teachings, we learn that God created the heaven and the earth and all things therein, making people and flowers the handwork of the same creator in the beginning. And plants, like humans, need the basic necessities — oxygen, water, and sunlight — to help sustain life.

In order to procreate the species, fertile seeds are necessary. In humans, it is the sperm from the male fertilizing the ovum from the female. In the flowers, it is the pollen dust from the anthers (the male part of the flower), fertilizing the pistils (the female part of the flower) of the same flower or others of its kind.

After fertilization of the flowers, fruits, nuts, or berries develop, and eventually the seeds will germinate under proper condition (soil, moisture, light), and produce new plants. The germinating and growing season is usually the spring in temperate climates, though in the tropics germination takes place any time of the year.

These plants mature steadily and gain strength and stability, and by summertime their buds have matured into hardy flowers, resplendent in their beauty and fragrance. For many flowers, the growing seasons have not been without mishap. Some get infested with diseases and insects such as aphids. Some get mowed down by ploughs and lawn mowers or trodden underfoot. Many of them are eaten by animals and birds, while others struggle to survive through droughts, floods, frost, and hailstones. Some flowers are cut and taken away to grace the tables and mantlepieces of homes or churches. Some form garlands for many and varied occasions. The survivors enjoy the cool, refreshing showers of sprinkling rain or heavy downpours, especially welcomed in the hot summer months, and they are admired by all.

The lucky ones remaining on their bushes or plants continue to grace the gardens, fields, and parks through the autumn of their lives. By then their colours begin to fade. The petals become limp and withered, and by wintertime they have all died, fallen off their plants, rotted and become nourishment for the soil, which next spring will again supply food for their plants, bushes, or germinated seeds, thus helping to sustain their life cycle.

So it is with humans. We grow from fertilized ovum incubated in the womb. We emerge in our springtime as babies. We blossom and grow through our summertimes into adulthood, experiencing many things along the way.

Just like the flowers, we have happy, sad, interesting, tragic, and enjoyable periods as we grow. And those of us who survive to see our autumns and winters can empathize with them because it is then that we begin to notice that we are no longer beautiful, strong, self-assured and capable as we were in the summers of our lives. As our winters approach, so too does the realization that we are approaching the end of our life cycles on the earth.

Thankfully though, through the process of reproduction, our species is able to continue life's seasonal journey, as our offspring continue where we have left off.

Oh! But if we could be like the flowers, accepting with grace and willingness the plight which we, like them, have no control over. It is our destiny, and destiny must be fulfilled.

The Joys of Summer

Summer is here, and so are all the fun (and not-so-fun) things that are associated with this torrid season.

Summertime is the season of the year that follows spring and precedes autumn. It extends from June 21 to September 23 in the northern hemisphere. However, the seasons are reversed in the southern hemisphere, therefore summer occurs from December 22 to March 21.

Summer is the season when average temperatures are highest, and periods of daylight are longest. In the northern hemisphere, the North Pole is most inclined towards the sun in the summer, therefore the intensity of the sun's heat is at its greatest on June 21, the longest day of the year in the northern hemisphere, and the longest night in the southern hemisphere. On December 22, the situation is reversed.

Although the intensity of the sun is greatest in late June in the Northern Hemisphere, the heat is absorbed by the earth, and is gradually released into the atmosphere. As a result hottest days of summer occur in August and the hottest month in the southern hemisphere is usually February.

Summer is the season that everyone looks forward to. Time for freedom from mundane tasks and boring jobs. A time when families seem to be able to do and enjoy certain things together, with more freedom and ease than could be afforded during other seasons, such as winter.

The great outdoors is the main arena. Everyone wants to be there to soak up the sun in varying amounts. The beaches during this season are usually busy places, as they are the doorsteps to the water, whether it is river, lake, sea, or pond. Water activities are many and varied, the most popular being swimming, water-skiing, canoeing, boating, or trying to land the "big one."

Many families go camping on weekends or for longer periods of time. They drag along their tents in backpacks, on top of their motor vehicles, or in their campers.

Day hikes and picnics are also favourite pastimes for those who cannot afford the time or money to be away for longer periods. But these sons and daughters of nature have so much to gain — so much to see and learn in the back woods of their journeys.

Nature is lush and in full bloom at this time of year. The trees are green and fully dressed. Their branches are living umbrellas for those who wish to dodge the scorching rays of the sun.

The grass and undergrowth in forests and woodlands are green and velvety underfoot. Wild flowers in profusion are everywhere, and match the ones in cultivated gardens with their beauty and fragrance.

Beautiful birds are everywhere, entertaining with their songs or just their presence. Wild animals rare and common can be seen, depending on the geography of one's travels.

Waterfalls and running streams are not only beautiful to behold on a hot summer's day, but cool, refreshing interruptions for hot and tired sojourners.

Some people plan summer trips, such as cruises, vacations on tropical islands, or an entire summer at the cottage. Close to home, some take to backyard camping in tents, or sleep under the stars.

Summers are very famous for fairs, festivals, and sporting events where people socialize, meet friends and acquaintances, and enjoy delicious foods. Some go on day trips, visit museums, exhibitions, and historic sites, or go back to school for summer courses.

Barbecuing is a summer norm and the industrious among us get the chance to make and serve not only the traditional lemonade and iced tea, but also such exotic and nutritious cooling drinks as carrot juice, coconut water, pineapple juice, and tropical fruit punch. Of course ice and ice-makers are necessities, and homes that do not have air conditioning have at least one oscillating fan.

Summer, however, has its drawbacks, like any other season. Some people get sick from too much exposure to the sun, a situation more prevalent nowadays because of the ozone layer depletion and the breaking down of earth's protective barrier shield against the sun's ultraviolet rays. Therefore sunstroke and heat prostration are common, but as people learn to moderate their exposure to the sun's rays, these incidences will decrease.

Traffic and water accidents are also common, but here, too, people need to be safety-conscious, considerate of others and less hurried when operating motor vehicles or watercrafts.

Summer brings bugs in abundance. Blackflies and mosquitoes are nuisances in campsites, wooded and swampy areas, as are ants and houseflies around our picnic sites.

Cutting our lawns and keeping them and our gardens well watered can be arduous, but many delight in these summer tasks.

Because of the amount of fluid our bodies lose through the process of perspiration, our fluid consumption is much higher in the summer than at any other season. It is also critical to pay attention to our salt intake.

In the summertime most people feel the need to relax and laze around more than in other seasons. This could be due to the physical draining of one's energy from the intense heat, or the fact that most people equate summer with relaxation, or both. Regardless of the reason, everyone craves a period of relaxation, and this craving seems to be satisfied mostly in the summertime.

Summer is a season of growth, development, perfection, and fulfillment, when most of us can get away with wearing very little and doing the same. Whether in the northern or southern hemisphere, summer will always be the season most people look forward to with great anticipation. A season to unwind. Oh! The joys of summer!

Ode to August

You are that month, August, when the summer sun's heat
Can cause us all to run around in our bare feet;
You make us want to stay for hours in the pool,
And enjoy the foods and drinks that will keep us cool.

Most of your days are torrid, so are your nighttimes too,
And your skies are often hazy, even though blue;
Rain is usually scarce, so terra firma is dry,
Evening times, when winter sun has set, yours is high.

August with your intense heat, you're precious, though
It may sap our strength, and our activities slow.
You are the height of summer in our northern climes,
In a season most folks crave for at other times.

August, eighth month of the year, for a king was named,
And like your zodiac sign, the lion, can't be tamed.
Yet in you beauty lies, just like your flowers and gems,
Depth in your peridot and strength in your poppies' stems.

And for the many famous things and people who
Are associated through history with you,
You're charted on the pages of time, as you should be.
August you're a very important month to me.

Midway through one of your sizzling days I first came,
Equipped with naught but newly-found freedom and a name.
Since then, all that you are, I have held on the line;
Whatever your reputation, August, you are mine.

Back to Scotland

I'm going back to Scotland for to recall old times,
And see once more friends that I have made in Scottish climes,
To walk again upon the pathways trodden by my feet,
And view the gorgeous landscapes that once my eyes did meet.
I will allow my mind to trip down memory lane again,
I'll feel the Scottish sunshine and walk in its summer rain.

To climb once more its scraggy hillsides and its coal bings,
Visit the gift shops that are brimming with Scottish things,
And then to roam the fields and the heather-fragrant vales,
And listen to the dialect and Highland tales.
To see Loch Lomond and maybe cruise on the River Clyde,
Stray up to Scourie's north shores and take in its ebb tide.

The highland cattle as they graze on hillsides and dells,
The trawlers with their scaly prize, riding the sea's swells
As they head for shore, all laden with their ocean-fresh catch,
While the buyers at the piers just simply wait and watch.
Granite-structured houses that glisten in Aberdeen
After the rain — nowhere else I have such beauty seen.

To buy vinegar-drenched fish and chips — what a treat!
And Mom's freshly baked scones, made just for me to eat.
Porridge with brown sugar, stovies and shepherd's pie:
Instead of saying "yes," I guess I will just say "aye!"

To hear the bagpipes play with zest those old Scottish reels,
And see the highland dancers as they kick up their heels.
See places that I knew, which there's no doubt, have changed,
And people whose lives, like mine, time has rearranged.
Remember things said and done then, through laughter and tears,
Kindness and love that mingled with all my joys and fears.
I will reach out for memories that have lived in my heart,
And going back to Scotland is a good place to start.

I Remember Scotland

I looked out the window of the aircraft, and the thick darkness that we had been flying through for the past eight hours was no longer evident. There was a moon, half full, and its light flooded the heavens.

I pulled the shutter down and looked back at the TV screen, trying to concentrate on the Grand Canyon documentary, but with little success.

I was excited, nervous, eager; and had been like that since the day dawned. I was going back to Scotland after thirty years. Ever since my friend Dahlia and I had decided to go back for a vacation, my mind had been on overdrive. I tried to recall in minute detail all the good and not-so-good times I had spent in Scotland as a pupil midwife at Bellshill Maternity Hospital.

I thought of all the wonderful people I had met and all the beautiful places in that country I had visited. I thought of the bings that flanked the back of MacDougal House where I lived; these are mounds formed from the residue of coal mining, some creating fair-sized hills, which eventually become overgrown with grass and shrubbery. Dahlia and I had climbed, explored, and sat on top of these bings on the many occasions when we had the need to overcome our homesickness, to while away the time, or to commune with nature.

I thought of busy Bellshill Square where I had shopped so many times. St. Thomas' Methodist Church in Coatbridge, the Baptist Church in Hamilton and the Tent Hall in Glasgow. These were places where I had worshipped and found the inner peace and contentment of being in the presence of God and His people. I also remembered the many picnic spots all over the country where our wonderful friends took us on so many occasions.

Memories of camping on the Trossachs for two days, having been taken there by the Mathesons, who supplied us also with the tent and food, and the cruises on the River Clyde and Loch Catherine. Then there were many visits to Loch Lomond, Edinburgh, and Aberdeen, where another friend, Elsie, lived.

Memories erupted like a volcano, but tumbled so quickly out of focus, I was unable to concentrate on any one scene long enough. But just then, as the moon smiled at me through the cabin window, my mind was lulled into a sense of tranquility and was no longer cluttered.

The difficulty my friend and I had at first understanding the Scottish accent and getting used to such terms as a piece (referring to a sandwich) wee (for "little"),and hen (referring to a woman) came back into my mind and encouraged a smile.

I remembered the first delivery that I saw. It was traumatic for all involved (the baby was grossly deformed and died a few minutes after), but I also remembered my first normal delivery, a beautiful baby girl, and how happy the first-time parents were at her birth.

I remembered my short nursing stints in the "pavilions," then moving into the glass-walled new hospital. I remembered the Queen's visit when she officially opened the hospital. I had just delivered a baby six hours before, and there he was, in his mother's arms. I remember how tender and soft the Queen's smile was as she looked at the baby, and I acknowledged that I was indeed the nurse who delivered him. I was so excited then to see the Queen at such close range and to have her speak to me. It was an experience of a lifetime, that I have thought of from time to time and will always remember.

I remembered my adventures with my friend when we hitchhiked to Scourie from Bellshill. I even remembered the long-handled collection plate that was passed down through the pews from the aisle of the little country church where we worshipped while in Scourie. We had giggled about how funny it looked, after we left the service. We had never seen anything like it before nor since, but we did agree that it was downright practical.

I remembered how difficult it was (and still is), to eat fish and chips from a newspaper wrapper, but also how delicious the taste of hot buttered scones from Mom Matheson's oven was and my love of Scottish shortbread.

I remembered the many times our friend Jan comforted us because we were homesick, or had a bad day in the classroom or on the ward. My first exposure to snow happened in Scotland and is another event etched in my memory. Then there was my first sight of highland cattle with their thick wooly coats.

I remembered the many dinners at the MacVicars and the sing-alongs around the piano afterwards. Memories like the picnics at the seaside and summer suns that lingered in the sky long past ten o'clock at nights came flooding back to me and it seemed like just yesterday instead of thirty years ago.

I remembered learning to drive in Scotland and the many practice runs Dad Matheson used to give me. He was so patient and kind, so much like a father to me. (Sadly I was not to see him on my return as he had passed on some years before.)

I was remembering with ease and I realized that the good memories outnumbered and outweighed the bad ones. Yes, there were a few bigoted ward sisters and midwives who tried to give my friend and me a hard time. Yes, there were ignorant people on the wards, on the buses, on the streets, in the banks and the stores, who would stare at us with contempt. And there was the woman with whom I boarded while doing my district rotation. She kept the house so cold I used to go to bed fully dressed and still shiver, and she fed me so poorly that I ended up having my evening meals at the Mathesons so I would have the strength to survive and do my work well.

There were many good, loving, and friendly people I was remembering. The Matron, many of the doctors, the District Midwives, and the wonderful families I was going back to visit — the Mathesons, the MacVicars, and Joan Stewart. They had helped to make my stay in Scotland enjoyable and worthwhile. We had kept in touch throughout the years, and going back to see them after thirty years was an anticipated joy.

I opened the window shade in the aircraft's cabin to its half mark and peered out, expecting to see the smiling moon again. The golden fringe on the horizon announced the dawn of day. I moved my watch forward past midnight into Greenwich Mean Time. It was now 6:00 a.m.

Once safely on Scottish soil, I realized quickly that not everything I remembered about Scotland was or would be the same. The airport in Glasgow, for instance, was a new one There were new highways and roundabouts, new shopping plazas and hotels, and there were no more coal bings. Areas that were once fields and farmlands were now built-up housing communities.

Double-decker buses were now a novelty in the areas that I visited. (I saw a few in Edinburgh, being used as tour buses for tourists.) Bellshill Maternity Hospital looked the same, but it was different. Many wards were vacant or closed and those in use were half-filled. The Matron had retired and lived near the hospital. Dr. Tennant and a few other doctors I had known had died. Pupil midwives were now being trained in community colleges, going to the hospital only for their practicum.

Since my visit and tour of my midwifery alma mater in 1994, I have learned with sadness that it has now been closed and may be turned into a hotel.

Remembering always brings to the foreground of one's mind incidents, situations, and encounters that were happy, sad, funny, unusual, pleasant, or unpleasant and that have so impressed one that they are readily recalled. For me, remembering Scotland was no exception.

As a Jamaican-trained registered nurse doing the midwifery course in Bellshill Maternity Hospital, I learned quickly that nursing is basically the same everywhere — although, for my friend and me, studying in a foreign country meant adjusting to the people, their accent, their culture, and the environment, and do it quickly, for survival's sake. We used our friendly personae and natural interest in people, places, and things to learn all we could about our environment. In so doing, we were exposed to incidents and situations which instilled in us laughter, love, sadness, concern, and understanding.

Incidents happened in the hospital setting as well as far afield. I remember a few days after our arrival in Bellshill, my friend and I went exploring in the town, after which we decided to walk back to the hospital as a way of getting used to the area. We had just started out on the Old North Road when we were offered a lift from a very tall driver in a very small car. We accepted and chatted amicably with the stranger, who asked us where we were from, why we were here, and why we had chosen Bellshill to study midwifery. We told him a bit about ourselves, and a lot about our country. He seemed very impressed with us, and by the time he dropped us off at MacDougal House, it was as if we had known him for years.

Five days later when classes had begun, in walked our "friend," being introduced to the class by the teacher as the Hospital Chief of Staff, Dr. Tennant. Needless to say that we were shocked to think that ordinary students like us had been chatting it up a few days ago with the hospital's Chief. We wondered if our forwardness would cause us trouble. It did not. The doctor is one of my lovely memories of Bellshill and Scotland.

Then there was the day I had just alighted from the bus on Old Monkland Road on my way to do a postnatal visit, when a little girl about seven years old ran up to me from the house beside the bus stop and said "Darkie Nurse! My mum say you're a darkie nurse!" I was of course taken aback, for although I had experienced rude stares and silent contempt from the general population, I had never been confronted like this before and I had certainly not heard the term "darkie nurse" before.

From the corner of my eye I noticed slight movements of the curtains that draped the window of the house from which the child had emerged. It was evident that the mother was hiding behind them, taking in the scene she had created.

I smiled at the girl and said, loudly enough for the eavesdropper to hear. "Your mother is very ignorant. Tell her she should get out more!" The words fell off my tongue easily, but there was no anger in my voice or in my heart. The child walked back into her yard and I continued on my way.

I remember, too, on my district rotation, my encounter with a four-legged friend. I had emerged from the house where I had just completed a delivery. The midwife had left a few minutes before, and since it was early in the afternoon of a fine day, I had decided to return to my digs via the bus instead of the customary taxi. I had walked past two houses and was about to cross the street to the bus stop when I saw him. He had jumped his fence and stood on the sidewalk looking at me. He had a brindled coat with black markings around his muzzle and looked fierce, as boxers usually do. I love dogs, and did not let his foreboding appearance daunt me.

"Gosh, you look like Bruce," I said, walking much slower now. Bruce was a boxer that my friends Alec and Agnes owned. I had been very wary when I first met Bruce because I had never encountered a boxer before, but it did not take me long to realize that he was a loving, friendly, and playful dog.

My new boxer wagged his stump of a tail, sat for a second, then trotted towards me. I stopped and smiled at him. He sniffed me, and licked my hands as I gently patted his head. I began walking again and he trotted beside me to the bus stop, where we waited for the bus. When the bus arrived and I got on it, he stood there looking after it until it was out of sight. For the next two-and-a-half weeks I had to be in the same neighbourhood, doing follow-up visits for other deliveries I had done. My boxer, as I called him, would wait for me at his gate, wagging his stump in greeting, walk with me to the bus stop, watch me board, then watch the bus until it was out of sight. I have often wondered how long he continued to watch for me after I had left the district. I have been partial to boxers ever since.

There was also the night when I was called to a delivery in the Town Head area of Coatbridge. The midwife and I arrived at about the same time and found that the very industrious husband had everything under control. There was a large pot on the stove boiling, the tea-kettle whistling, a nice fire going in the fireplace in the living room, the delivery bed made up with clean linen, and the patient bathed and ready.

Before long the patient was delivered of a beautiful baby girl and the rest of the delivery continued smoothly. After its expulsion from the uterus, I placed the placenta (afterbirth) into a bowl and put it aside for a more complete examination after I had cleaned up the mother and bathed the baby. (It is very important that the placenta is examined thoroughly to make sure that none of its lobes or membranes remain in the mother's uterus, as this could cause severe haemorrhaging infection or both).

When I was ready to examine the placenta, it was not where I had placed it, nor could it be found. I inquired of the husband if he had put it someplace else.

"Oh!" he said looking a bit puzzled that we would be asking after it. "I gave it to the dog. I didn't want a nice piece of meat like that to go to waste!"

After we recovered from the shock of the moment, we explained to him why it was important that the placenta was properly examined. He was very apologetic but I had to visit the mother twice a day for a week and a half to make sure she was not bleeding or showing signs of infection. After that incident, I made sure to examine the placenta as soon as it is delivered, and if that was not possible for whatever reason, I always asked that it be left alone until I said that it could be disposed of. I have laughed at that incident many times since.

On another occasion, I was doing a postnatal visit of a baby boy I had delivered two days before. The mother had the baby stripped and lying on the sofa in the living room, which was warmed by the fire in the fireplace. The mother had just taken me two steps away into the kitchen so I could wash my hands before handling the baby. Then suddenly the baby started screaming and so did three-year-old Alison, who was shouting "Mummy! It won't come off! It won't come off!"

We dashed into the room to find that she had her baby brother's genitalia firmly in her grasp and was pulling with all her might. I put a compress on the baby's genitalia and we took him into hospital to make sure he was okay. He was. We explained to his sister that little boys are made that way.

I had a wonderful vacation in Scotland in 1994. I revisited old haunts, as well as new places. Met with old and dear friends and made new ones. I reminisced about old experiences and lived new ones. I enjoyed then, as I had before, the beautiful ruggedness of Scotland, the warm and wonderful fellowship of my friends, and the depth of their love and friendship.

I remembered. I still remember and will always remember Scotland with warmth and caring and love, for as long as I live.

Of Lochs and Bings

I do remember Scotland as a land of lochs and bings
Of bluebells, thistle, heather, Gaelic, and Highland flings.
Of hazy skies in winter, red sun, and cold, dry days;
Extended hours of summer, crowded with fun always.

Of castles old and crumbling, or nobly occupied,
And double-decker transports, which between cities plied.
Of Camberslang and Glasgow, Scourie and Aberdeen,
And Bellshill Hospital, where I once spoke to the Queen.

And when I think of Scotland, I see mountains and hills,
Rivers that offer hydro power to woollen mills;
See Highland cattle grazing in heather-dotted fields,
Farmers at harvest gathering whatever the soil yields.

I think with warmth and love when I gaze in Lomond's deep,
At the Northern Lights and Scotland's woolly sheep.
On cool spring morns when magpies call and a robin sings,
I do remember Scotland when I think of lochs and bings.

Bluebells and Heather — 1

Bluebells, how beautiful you'd look
Inside warm indoor gardens
Each winter, when earth hardens,
And ice forms on river and brook.
Then we'd not lose the sight of you
For frost has dulled your gorgeous blue.

And heather, gracing hills and moors,
Could I perhaps entice you,
To leave the outside world too,
And come and live with me indoors?
I guess not, for you are a child
Of nature, and you must stay wild.

So I will have to be content,
Bluebells and heather, always
Enjoy you on summer days,
And hoard your beauty and sweet scent,
To last me through each winter rain,
Till spring and summer come again.

Bluebells and Heather — 2

A cheery sight to see always,
In pleasant Scottish weather;
Gracing the hills on summer days,
Are the bluebells and the heather!

Warm summer breezes' subtle kiss,
Blows against stem so tender.
I can't resist a sight like this;
I to the charms surrender.

Bluebells' and heather's perfumes blend,
And paint the air unseeing.
Beauty on sight and smells does lend
Awe and joy to God's beings.

Hillside Jewel

O Scottish flower, you are to me,
A precious gem, of rare beauty.
Where did you get your colours bright?
Were you perhaps dipped in the full moon's light?
Then left to glow on the Scottish hill,
And show your charm against the birds' own trill?
I bet it is so, for nowhere on earth
Is another like you, or with your worth.

To me you are beautiful as can be,
Would that I could take you back across the sea,
So in my eyes you could always shine,
Thou pearl of the hillside, jewel, mine.
But my mind must hold your beauty rare,
If my eyes cannot with ardour stare
At your dazzling form, as you sway and tease
My convincing mind in the Scottish breeze.

A Touch of Frost

A touch of frost is in the air, a true indication that summer, and all the joys and ease that go with it, is over. All the lazy days and frolics, the early-morning and late-night walks, the gardening and bird watching are put on hold for six months as we look towards the cooler seasons of autumn and winter and all they offer.

Many annual fall activities have been completed. These activities would seem aberrant if a touch of frost in the air were lacking. Oktoberfest and grape festivals go hand in hand with fall and cool weather. And frost nips many pumpkins in Southern Ontario even as we celebrate Thanksgiving Day.

Halloween trick-or-treaters have to withstand the proverbial nip of Jack Frost's presence in the air as they parade from door to door, charming or scaring goodies out of generous householders.

It is that time of year when frost is expected as well as tolerated. Frosty days have to be tolerated. There is nothing one can do except to cancel one's outdoor activities and stay indoors, where hopefully it is warm. Not many are willing to do that, however. There are too many exciting things to see and do outdoors even on frosty days.

Most people living in the northern hemisphere find the colder seasons of the year challenging; and, come the first frost of autumn, they are ready and willing to rise to the many challenges they face. They even manage to enjoy them. They look forward to their skiing trips on snowy slopes, ice or street hockey, skating on frozen ponds and lakes as the north wind whips naked faces, causing unprotected cheeks and noses to blush red unwillingly.

Fishermen abandon their boats of summer and move to holes dug through frozen lakes and rivers. This is a continuation of the feat started in the summer, and their deep desire to get the "big one." Most of the time though, is spent hopping around and rubbing hands together to keep warm, if they are not fortunate enough to have warm huts over their holes.

Such people are darned if they would allow a touch of frost, or snow or ice or cold, to daunt their desire to do the things they want to do, where and when they want to do them. They are determined to enjoy life while there is life to enjoy, whatever the season, or climatic conditions.

A touch of frost in the air is a sign of many things to many people. For farmers, it is a time to harvest the apples and pears and grapes. It means the migration of birds to warmer southern climes. This includes the human "snowbirds," although I suspect that some may be deterred because of our slumping dollar, and the new health insurance law that will affect them if they move south of the border for the winter.

A touch of frost means that our winter clothing is brought out of storage and readied for use. Our motor vehicles, now winterized and snow-tire-clad, are ready for hard winter days ahead. Furnaces are checked and made ready to assure the householders of adequate heating when it is required. Summer furniture is once again put away in garden sheds or basements.

We prepare our minds and bodies for such mundane things as shovelling snow from walks and driveways, scraping frost from our windscreens, and making sure that we have in our pockets or handbags those little containers of lock de-icer.

Once again, soon the beautiful trees which we have been admiring, painting, and photographing all summer, will lose their leaves (except the evergreens of course!). We will rake, burn, bag and compost these leaves, and be content to gaze through colder months, at the trees' naked and ghost-like branches. Then one day next spring, as we welcome new life around us and the return of our feathered friends, we'll most likely have forgotten the first frosty day that ushered in autumn and winter, because we are not intimidated by a touch of frost.

Is It That Time Again?

The days are getting shorter and the sun now seems to set
Much earlier than it did a month ago.
Now dawn comes much later and days remain quite warm, but yet
The dull, low sky seems to have lost its glow.
There occasionally is cold rain,
Oh! Could it be that time again?

Mornings are mute, have all the birds gone off to southern skies?
Has wild birds' nesting season ended now?
Will the heaven remain voiceless, devoid of the blue jays' cries?
The robin, is he gone from yonder bough?
Are the green leaves now turning brown?
Are summer tourists leaving town?

I am not sure if wafer-thin ice is what I saw
Crusting the puddles formed from midnight rain.
Perhaps it was that I dreamed warm sunlight did the crystals thaw,
And rid the sod of moisture once again.
Is my neighbour covering his pool?
Have children gone back to school?

Do I detect a hint of frost in the October air
When I go out at nights for my brisk walks?
Or am I really raking leaves that fall from everywhere?
Don't I realize that nearby winter stalks?
I am wishing, but it's in vain,
It's definitely that time again.

'Tis the Season

December has again arrived and the temperature has dropped. The wind blows colder, the days are shorter, and the darkness of the nights appears to be so much deeper.

As the month matures we find ourselves moving towards the festive season of Christmas. The time of year when joy, mirth, laughter, and music resound, and beautiful decorations inside and outside our houses, cities, villages, and towns are the norm. The same can be said for feasting, festivities, and gift giving.

Christmas, a holiday (or holy day) throughout the Christian world, is the anniversary of the giving of love. The love of God, given to the world through the birth of Christ our Saviour, in a far-away Bethlehem manger a long, long time ago. The event, in Christendom, establishes the immeasurable love of God for mankind.

In our present-day world, this love is almost forgotten, except where it affects us ourselves. Christmas has become, to most, a season for merrymaking, getting a new wardrobe, going on a lavish vacation to some warm, exotic spot, roasting a thirty-pound turkey or ham (or both), and feasting with our relatives and friends.

In these hard economic times, the people who can take part in these kinds of revelling are obviously from the ranks of the wealthy. They have been blessed by birth or fate or luck, and will not know the iron hardship of poverty, job redundancy, or the hardship of the sick and aged poor. Some of these poor will look back at last Christmas and see their lot mirrored before their eyes. There has been no change, except for the worse. Others have joined the ranks of the have-nots for the first time. This year, they have watched their sources of income vanish with the closing of plants and factories and the downsizing of numerous businesses. They watched their hopes and dreams for the future being dashed to pieces before their eyes, and there was nothing they could do about it.

Many of our poor are victimized further by the present government's attitude towards their situation. The introduction of workfare and the severe cutbacks in welfare payments have rendered the plight of some hopeless. For all of these people, Christmas is the season for hunger, cold, want, fear, desperation, disappointment, and depression.

The lines at food banks and soup kitchens are overextended now, and many shelters have to turn people away. The contents of the food bank larders are few, sometimes nonexistent. Much is needed in the form of food, clothing, toys, money, and our time. We can volunteer our time to help collect, sort, prepare, and deliver kindness and caring to those in need of it, and we need to do it with a smile, good spirits, and love in our hearts. In so doing, we can have the joy that Christmas is supposed to bring, and know that we have helped someone in need along the way.

Let us make it a season of hope, love, and caring. A season of giving our time to the lonely, the sick, the needy, the troubled, the depressed. A time of understanding the urgent needs of the less fortunate, and giving and sharing what we have, however small it may be. Let us give our love — a very dynamic thing. For with the giving of love, all else will fall into place. If there is love, then there will be giving and sharing, compassion and peace — all the ingredients needed to make for a happy Christmas season.

Yes, 'tis the season for cleaning and decking the halls, and trimming and decorating the trees, but that is not all. 'Tis also the season for remembering the poor, the dispossessed, all those who have lost their freedom for political, religious, or cultural reasons. 'Tis the season for love to shine from us, as did the love of God through the Christmas Star, that long-ago night in Bethlehem.

'Tis the season for Love and Giving and Peace!

'Tis the Season

'Tis the season for giving
All that we have and can give.
'Tis the season for living,
And allowing others to live.

'Tis the season of plenty
For the world's rich all around.
But for the million and twenty
Have-nots, poverty is what they have found.

'Tis the season when all should
Learn of the peace and the joy.
That Christmas love in each heart could
Make someone's day, love employ.

'Tis the season love should flow
Freely, like waters unchecked.
'Tis the season love should grow,
Even if our halls are not decked.

'Tis the season when love brings
Us all the feeling of peace.
We need not have the gifts of kings;
Loving will our larders increase.

'Tis the season of blessings,
For everyone who believes.
Though we feast not on rich dressings,
Love is the gift each receives.

What is Left After Christmas?

What is left after the highs of the Christmas season is over? Most of us who have a job to go to have returned and resumed some normality of everyday life. The children have returned to school, some reluctant to leave behind their newly acquired toys and or video games.

Christmas trees, which only days ago were resplendently dressed and aglow with tinsel, lights, and bows, are now either packed away in their boxes for another year, or are lying pathetically at the bottom of driveways and at the edges of winter-brown lawns, waiting to be hauled away unceremoniously in the bellies of garbage trucks already swollen with the other leftovers from the Christmas festivities. Christmas decorations are taken down and returned to that sacred nook in the basement or attic. And the few outdoor decorations left will remain where they are until spring or next December.

The turkey is all used up, even the bones, which made some delicious soups. The good tablecloths are folded and put away. And the bills have started to come in.

The echoes of "Joy to the World," and "Peace, Goodwill to Men," have faded fast. But should things be this way? Should not the spirit of Christmas linger in our hearts, our homes, and our world from December to December? We should still feel the warmth and love that was so generously shared with friends, families, neighbours, workmates and strangers during the Christmas season. This warmth, love, and generosity should continue to radiate to and through each one of us long after Christmas is over.

What is left after Christmas should not be the humdrum of a long cold miserable winter, but a New Year filled with hope and warmth and love. Hope for a revived, vibrant, and healthy economy. Love and compassion for each other, the abundance of peace within ourselves, in our nation and our world.

I hope that the joys and blessings we might have experienced the Christmas season, continue through the new year. After all, we can but hope!

A happy, safe, and healthy New Year to all of us!

A Time for Reflection

With every New Year comes a deep desire for a better, more prosperous and fulfilling year than the one we left behind.

After the revelries of the holiday season are past and the feasts and festivities over, we settle down (or ought to) and reflect upon the year that has just passed and ponder the one now unfolding.

In these unsettling times, there is a lot to ponder and reflect on. Come this time next year, will we be in our jobs (those of us who have them)? Will we be able to shelter, clothe, and feed our families? Will we be able to afford and enjoy the social and medical security that we have worked towards putting in place and maintaining all our working lives, or will they be no more?

Will we continue to enjoy freedom fought for and won by many on the battlefields, on reservations and on the streets? Or will we find our bodies, souls and minds fettered in the warring dungeons of our desperate world? And what's more, will we even be alive?

For many, reflections constitute a time of anxiety and fear. It can be a great burden, this thing called reflection, because not always is it of good and happy thoughts and events, especially not in these times of hardships, disillusionment, and disappointments. Therefore it is wise for us to be calm, serene, and sensible in our reflections, and never allow our spirits to be trampled to the ground because fate has been unkind and no one seems to care.

We do not want to give in to defeat and fatalism. We have to battle the urge to give in to frustration and instead reflect on how things used to be and how they can be again. This will give us the courage and determination to continue up the steep inclines of time, persevering all the way until we reach the top.

Yes, at this time each year, people are bent on making resolutions and positive promises, hoping they will be able to stick to them. May everyone's future aspirations be positive ones, may our economy be pulled out of the doldrums of yesteryear, giving everything and everyone a chance to recover. And may all our secret dreams come true, especially those we have for our children and theirs.

A happy and prosperous New Year to all, with peace and love always.

New Year's Wishes for All

My wish for everyone as we embark on a New Year,
Is for lots of understanding and for lives devoid of fear.
For more neighbourly behaviour, each one helping each one live,
Good relationships with those at odds with us, as we forgive.

For strength to bear those burdens we cannot escape or change,
And to deal with disappointments and ideas that are strange.
Determination to push onwards, no thoughts of giving up,
Or being fearful, hesitant, even though bitter is the cup.

More cheerfulness in each household, may plenty reign again,
Economical revival to ease all financial strain.
The desire in all to work hard so as to improve our lot,
Remembering to be grateful for what we have already got.

For courage that we might need to propel us on our way
As we strive to conquer hardships we may face each waking day.
The ability to look ahead and a sound future plan,
And the faith and confidence we need to tell us that we can.

Love abundantly displayed, as each heart is opened wide
To embrace the strangers we may meet, to welcome them inside
Our hearts and our lives, a kinder attitude to show,
And the quest for knowledge, because what we are is what we know.

Happiness abundant and joyful times to linger on,
Continuing thus to flourish long after the year is gone.
That whatever odds we might encounter be what we can bear —
These are just a few sincere wishes for all of us, next year.

About the Author

A registered nurse and certified midwife, Linda M. Brissett worked in neonatology at the Henderson General Hospital in Hamilton, Ontario, for twenty-eight years. She served on the Board of Directors of the Afro-Canadian Caribbean Association of Hamilton and District and on the Seniors' Advisory Committee for Revenue Canada for four years each. She is a member of the Hamilton Health Sciences Corporation Quarter-Century Club, the Jamaica Foundation, the Canadian Poetry Association, and an Honorary Appointee to the Research Board of Advisors of the American Biographical Institute. She is a volunteer with Hamilton Tele-Touch and works on the Outreach Committee of Mt. Hamilton United Church.

Other publications are three books of poetry — *In Fields of Dream (and other poems), Sunshine in the Shadows*, and *Give Us This Day* — and a book of short stories, *Carols of Christmases Past*. She has contributed to the anthologies *The First Time* and *Ingots*, and has written many articles for the periodicals *The Bulletin* and *Authors*.

Linda lives in Hamilton, Ontario with her husband Louis and son Ian.